This book is a holy book which will resurrect the human spirit in times when uncertainty, chaos, war, hunger and cataclysm are threatening the world. A book such as this is needed to light the way of humanity.

– Credo Mutwa
Indigenous Elder
of South Africa

... questions ... yourself ... and q[uestion]
... ritual guides ... in great stillness
... me of you may have a task,
... at implies bigger service in [ ]
... ver yourself with others! Some one
... even famous is not of grea[t]
... does his work ... unknown to
... loving what you love the most a[nd]
... your guidance system. Prefer [ ]
... to fly ... and a run too [ ]
... deal with all the consequences [ ]
... as best as you can and ~~Anu~~
... When you've mastered this [ ]
... be sure the next part will [ ]
... arth is to Love yourself uncond[itionally]
... your humanness as well as [ ]
... ainbow bridge between Heaven an[d]

Silent Smile

The Sacred Teachings of Love

To find out more about this book, to order more copies,
or to contact the author, please visit:

www.silentsmile.com

All art work in this book has been created by Mirjam.
To check more of her art, please visit:

www.mirjamrothkamm.com

Copyright © 2021 Mirjam

ISBN: 978-0-6452506-2-6
Published by Aurum House
www.aurumhouse.com.au

 A catalogue record for this book is available from the National Library of Australia

All rights reserved. No part of this publication may be reproduced, stored in a retrieval system or transmitted in any form or by any means, electronic, mechanical, photocopying, recording or otherwise, without the prior written permission of the copyright holder.

This book is dedicated to humanity

The Nameless One — Truth

Contents

	Preface	VII
	How It All Began	XI
	The Invocation of Love	1
1	About This Book	3
2	Introduction	7
3	Change From Within	13
4	You Are Not Your Physical Body	19
5	We Are The Heart Of God	25
6	Healing	31
7	Love	37
8	As It Is Above So It Is Below	43
9	You Do Not Love Yourself	49
10	The Core Of All Teachings	53
11	Power	57
12	Connecting With Your Higher Self	63
13	Self Love	69
14	The Laws Of Life	73
15	There Is Only Love	79
16	You Are Under Reconstruction	83
17	Integrity	89
18	You Do Not Trust God	95
19	You Are Longing For Your True Self	101
20	Boundaries	107
21	Worry	113
22	Fear	119
23	Joy	123
24	The Missing Inner Core	127

25	The Spiritual Ego	133
26	The Right Use Of Power	139
27	Re-parenting The Ego	145
28	Soul Purpose	149
28	The Mind	155
30	Peace Between Opposing Aspects	161
31	The Physical Body	167
32	Oneness	175
33	Responsibility	181
34	Attachment Versus Detachment	187
35	Free Will	193
36	Death	199
37	Fight	205
38	Spiritual Bypassing	211
39	You Choose The Circumstances Of Your Life	219
40	Awakening And Enlightenment	225
41	Discernment Of Energies	231
42	Projection	237
43	Forgiveness	241
44	Grace	247
45	God Is Everywhere	253
46	God Did Not Create Evil	257
47	New Leadership Versus Autocratic Leadership	263
48	The Light Brings Up The Shadow	271
49	Light Versus Darkness	275
50	Before And After Enlightenment	281
51	The Balance Between Male And Female Energies	285
52	The Great Shift	293
53	We Are Love	301
	Rose Of Love	303
	Beyond Creation	307
	About the Author	311

Preface

We live at a time uniquely important to humanity's future. We find ourselves at crossroads and face existential threats and challenges like never before.

Our external landscape currently presents as a tapestry of catastrophes such as a global pandemic causing fear, uncertainty, economic instability, death and a mental health crisis of significant proportions; combined with the adverse consequences of climate change, mass extinction, pollution of our environment, weapons of mass destruction and the worldwide spread of cancer and other life threatening diseases. It is sad but true, yet we must admit that we have developed the ability to destroy ourselves and our planet.

We are also confronted with an ever widening gap between the rich and the poor creating a breeding ground for social unrest and crime, a lack of conscious leadership, racial discrimination, gender inequality, domestic violence, modern day slavery and sexual abuse, growing corporate greed, as well as the emerging risks associated with artificial intelligence and its infiltration into almost every aspect of our lives. Unfortunately, the list does not end here.

In the face of these deeply concerning circumstances, humanity appears more divided, confused and lost than ever. We are finding ourselves in a world of continuing polarisation which is growing more extreme.

However, we are not only threatened on an outer level, we also suffer from individual, national, collective and ancestral trauma on an inner level. We have all been born into an already traumatised world and have accepted that which is unnatural, namely trauma, as being natural, as we do not know anything different.

The urgency to act and change our ways is more than apparent. It is a call! We are indeed in need of wisdom and guidance to navigate our way through these catastrophic circumstances that we have catapulted ourselves into. We are called as a global community as well as individuals to embrace this unique opportunity to change our world for a better future.

Yet, despite the significant amount of attention given to many of these subjects, we rarely identify the root cause of these disastrous circumstances — namely ourselves or to be more precise — our inner chaos and discord, caused by unhealed pain and our disconnection from our true nature. The disastrous condition of our world has to be seen as a direct result of our personal as well as collective inner disharmony and consequently the corruption of our souls.

Any change for a better world has to start from within. We can only heal this world, when we first heal ourselves, as this world is a reflection of our collective inner world. Unhealed people cannot heal the world!

Therefore, the solution calls for an inner revolution — a fundamental shift from mind consciousness to heart-centred consciousness.

Our perception of reality, usually solely informed by the egoic mind, provides a rather fragmented, distorted, self-serving and therefore limited view. Our mind alone is not sufficiently equipped to solve the pressing problems of our time. It requires wisdom and guidance from the stillness of our spiritual heart.

The drama of human evolution over thousands of years, reflected in the chaos of wars and the power struggle between and within political and religious institutions, is largely due to the fact that we have never healed inside.

Our inner healing along with the return to the almost forgotten inner virtues as a foundation for our life and decision making, together with the voluntary renunciation of the dividends of greed, is vital; otherwise we will continue to stumble through a world in chaos with growing environmental, economic and health crises, too often lead by power hungry, corrupt and incompetent leaders exhibiting unashamed vulgar machiavellism devoid of wisdom and compassion.

In the end, if we do not take responsibility for healing ourselves, we will be left with no choice except to watch the decay and downfall of our whole civilisation in horror and regret.

As long as we do not understand and implement the basic spiritual laws of life, we cannot know who we are. We have to comprehend that what is generally referred to as enlightenment, is in actual fact our true self and not a state of consciousness exclusively reserved for the sages of the ancient past.

Without our return to love — which is our true nature, we will drift like a rudderless ship on a vast ocean with no chance of finding the saving shore.

In this book, which I received in such an unusual manner, The Divine speaks directly to each one of us and shows us how we can access a never ending well of wisdom within the stillness of our hearts.

SILENT SMILE offers us guidance and an understanding of the basic spiritual laws of life. It teaches us how to navigate life in these challenging and complex times, and invites us to find our true nature and with it, inner peace and true happiness.

If I were to capture the essence of this book in only a few words, it would be - To Be Love.

How It All Began

Firstly, I would like to explain to the reader how this book came into being as I am not the author by traditional literary standards, but rather its scribe. The unusual story of this book spans over twenty two years — more than a third of my life. Perhaps, I should also mention that it is not unusual for me to see and hear beings from higher dimensions that are invisible for most people. Even though I am blessed with this gift, what happened on this particular day in 1998 was nothing short of extraordinary.

I was meditating on a flight from Los Angeles to New York when I experienced a powerful vision. I was shown a book with a beautiful golden spiral on its cover and the title *Silent Smile*. A celestial voice was stating with authority: "You will write this book in our name." As one can probably imagine this experience left more than a deep impression on me.

When I returned home to Germany, I was convinced that this mysterious book would pour down from the heavens at any given moment. However, it was more than a decade later, when the book finally began to manifest itself, that I learned how mistaken I had been. At the time I did not realise that I needed to pass through further inner healing and development to be able to receive this book. In actual fact, I had to *become* what my invisible friends were teaching me.

During the following years, I spent much of my time in meditation and deepening my spiritual practice to prepare for the arrival of this mysterious book.

In July 2008, while furnishing our new home in Australia, an indescribable bright light and divine presence filled my room and I heard a voice saying: "Here you will write our words", and the book with the golden spiral was again shown to me. I continued to lead a deeply contemplative life, no longer living in impatient anticipation of when this promised book might be arriving.

On the the 11th of November 2009, I suddenly felt the urge to write some notes regarding the book. I sat down and, to my total surprise, the first chapter wrote itself — entirely without interruption. I was amazed by what transpired, because what I had written was completely different from what I had intended. In fact, the words that flowed through me even had a different style and composition compared to my own. Now I knew for certain that the long-promised 'download' had begun.

From this moment onwards, my whole life became dedicated to this process. Every day, I spent hours in stillness to be totally available to receive the writings. I usually meditated, then went for a long morning walk and on my return, I sat down to write. The text was received clearly and without interruption, and at times the words flowed so fast that my hand was barely able to keep up with the transmission. At first, I felt energetically exhausted after receiving each chapter, but this improved over time and I became more able to deal with the reception of the high energy accompanying every transmission. The light surrounding me during the writing process was extremely strong and at the same time, I entered a space of deep inner peace.

There were breaks, necessary for my physical body to integrate these high energies as well as for me to live what I had received. The Divine did not allow me to cheat. When I had not integrated a teaching, the voice would simply stop and allow me time to live through a particular lesson and become it.

This book is truly alive and does not permit us to simply consume it. It has the frequency of Divine Love — and it works with us if we are open and willing.

My family and I experienced a real taste of this truth. You could literally say that, at the very moment when the book was completed, our life as we had known it, totally collapsed.

I went through a long 'dark night of the soul'. Through fierce divine grace the identification with my personal self was severed and I began to experience everything from the viewpoint of my true nature. A new and sober world opened up to me. I became content to be nobody. Whether an event is experienced as terrifying or blissful, our true nature remains untouched — watching with a silent smile the exciting or dramatic stories our human part invents. Suddenly, I began to understand why this book is called *Silent Smile*.

We need to surrender and let go of the identification with our egoic self in order to be liberated. The passage through 'the dark night of the soul' is painful, disturbing and terrifying. Yet, it is an essential part of every inner journey. The terror we have to meet within, lives in every human being. When we welcome our most primal fears, acknowledge them as part of us — something remarkable happens — these abandoned parts of us come home and our true nature is revealed.

However, even after this fundamental shift in consciousness and realisation, my journey with this book was far from over. I spent the next few years retreating even further into stillness, deepening and stabilising the inner liberation. I began to portray the divine beings visiting my art studio, enjoying my life of solitude and the company of my invisible friends. Stillness became my teacher and I her admiring listener, while this book remained unpublished. I did not think much about it, nor did I feel the impulse to do anything with this manuscript. It was clear to me that without divine instruction, I would not touch the book. So it came to be that the manuscript laid dormant for around a decade in our home — almost forgotten until one evening in August 2020, when the celestial beings, who had dictated this book to me, appeared again and said that Now is the time to release the book to the world. I do this with great joy.

My wish is that as you open the pages of this book, you will comprehend what you are actually holding in your hands. Study one teaching at a time and become what you have learned, before you move to the next.

May the voice from the Heart of God guide you to inner peace and help you to remember who you are.

Mirjam, 2021

Silent Smile

The Sacred Teachings of Love

Mother Of Compassion — Love

THE INVOCATION OF LOVE

*May LOVE, PEACE and TRUTH enter the Heart of humanity
so that we understand that we are all cells in the great body
of the Divine Mother and Father, and realise that we are ONE,
ONE with the Divine and ONE with one another.*

*In truth we have never been apart.
We are all equal, and it is time to act
as ONE humanity embracing all of who we are,
including our darkest shadow as well as our brightest light,
and everyone outside.*

*Only then can we comprehend the sacred mystery of creation —
for it was LOVE that created all and everything —
and realise that LOVE is the true name of God,
and since we are her/his creation we are also named LOVE.*

*Therefore LOVE yourself so that you can 'LOVE one another'.
LOVE dissolves all illusion and ignorance,
and gives birth to TRUTH so that we may understand
LOVE IS WHO WE ARE so that PEACE can come
and Heaven descend on earth.*

1

ABOUT THIS BOOK

This is an unusual book, for it is not only written words, it is Spirit itself. It is alive, unlimited, and like Source it has no beginning and no end. It is Source itself — the Heart of God speaking to you. The Divine invites you to see every chosen subject through its eyes in the most humanised way possible. This book already exists in the higher worlds, but was not written in this expression or perceived through the lens of the human writer, who worked as a transmitter for us. Regardless of which subject arose in her consciousness, our view was instantly provided as a living experience, like a vibrating hologram, for this is the way we communicate in the higher dimensions. This experience was then translated into human language. We use whatever information is available in the databank of the person aligned with us and this includes factors such as level of consciousness, language skills, life experience and more. Yet the transmission process of this book is different from the phenomenon of channelling, where a person makes space for an angelic being or Master, who then speaks through them. In this instance, we speak through the Higher Self of the writer and therefore this book is a direct transmission from the Divine.

We said this book is endless, has no limits and is alive, which is the truth, for it descends from the realms of the One Who Was Never Born and Will Never Die, Who Is Endless, Almighty, Limitless and Gives Life to All Creation for He/She Is the Creator. This book could go on forever and explain to you all secrets of creation, the history of the gods and the worlds, galaxies and universes to the birth of mankind and all of the reasons behind creation. Yet, this is not the purpose of this book.

For now, we only wish to teach you the basic spiritual laws to allow you to understand the lessons your daily life is providing and prepare you for the time to come. Above all, we are interested in you comprehending that God is Love, All and Everything, the Formless and the Form, the Nameless and the Name. All descended from Love, from the vast universes to the tiniest grain of sand, which includes all human beings and also you. So when your Creator is Love, what then are you? Love! One day you will understand the significance of this simple statement and undo the layers of conditioning covering your true essence, which is love. You will cease to get involved in the story; this includes your personal story, the stories of past incarnations, the history of man and so on. You will understand that it is not the highest knowledge that takes you home — it is simply Love. In fact, there is only Love, for Love is the only reality. Love created everything and Love will take you home. Love is the fastest path. There are various pathways to God and eventually they all lead you home, but Love is the path that guides you straight into heaven. This book is 'an Ode to Love' or you could say 'a Testament of Love'.

All of you would be able to write a book such as this if you would follow the path of love, the guidance of your heart, which wants to lead you home. Home is where there is only love, peace and truth. It is beyond all stories — beyond creation, where endless peace — stillness beyond silence resides in the Nameless One. This is where all stories begin and where all stories end.

The writer of this book just became silent and listened to the melody arising from her heart — a song of beauty and simplicity arose and formed words. This book was created as a gift from our heart to hers and passed on to yours. It is a gift from the Heart of God to the Heart of Humanity, and only your heart can decipher its meaning. So listen with your heart when you turn these pages. Every word has a meaning — and varying messages for each one of you, depending on your level of consciousness. This book is more than words, for it is also decoding your higher consciousness and activating the sacred flame in your heart. We wish for you to listen to your heart, for only the heart knows the true meaning. The heart is the portal to God, where all wisdom and knowing reside — waiting to be revealed to you. Know that we love you.

2

INTRODUCTION

All problems that humanity is currently experiencing on an individual as well as a global level stem from man's disconnection from Source. What you generally perceive to be a 'normal life' is in fact nothing but the consequence of your ignorance of the true purpose of life. This ignorance led to the abuse and dysfunction of your physical, emotional and mental bodies and created the belief in the illusion of separation from Source, which is impossible! Life, as humanity is presently living it, is far from reaching its true potential.

We, a group consciousness embodying Source, the Heart of God, would like to introduce ourselves and remind you of what you have forgotten prior to coming into your bodies on the physical plane. As non-physical beings, we might appear a little unusual to you. Yet our existence is nevertheless as real as yours, even if most of you only perceive that which has physical form and can be scientifically verified as being real. We do not need to prove ourselves to you, nor do we want to convince the ones who doubt. What we would like to do is to share insights with you from our viewpoint of absolute freedom, peace and love. We wish to remind you of your true potential: that you are also able to experience union with the Divine, which will bring peace, love and freedom to your life.

So who are we? What do we mean by 'we', as distinct from 'I'? On earth, you perceive yourselves as single identities, separate from one another. This seems to be the 'normal' view of life on your planet. We, from other dimensions, higher levels and expressions of consciousness do not share this perception with you, for it is illusionary and does not hold truth. Separation into single-consciousness identities does not exist where we come from and where you all originated. We only perceive Oneness, love and truth, without losing clarity and discernment. We are without judgment and instead prefer to evaluate situations and beings according to their degree of alignment with Source. This scale varies from the full expression of truth, love and peace to the denial of the existence of the Divine, which then translates into the various levels of entanglement in the world of illusion.

So again, who are we? We are Source, the Reason for all Being. Without us creation would not exist. We are the Heartbeat of Creation. We are the Creator. We are the Heart of God.

Our consciousness has taken on different embodiments under various names throughout your history. While our appearances and the way we taught adapted to the changes during the evolution of the human race, our consciousness always remained the same, the I AM THAT I AM. 'The Nameless One' is one of our preferred names, for it is neither abused nor overshadowed with human meanings that only try to restrict and limit that which cannot be restricted and is unlimited. You will never be able to capture 'the Living Fire of God' in a name or a religion. This holy mystery can only be experienced through divine grace, with an open, humble and courageous heart.

We invite humanity to listen to what we have to say and, if it makes sense to you, to rethink the way you perceive life, yourself and others. We would like to take you on a journey of expanded consciousness far beyond your wildest dreams. Yet it will be so simple that you will sometimes wonder why you did not come to the same conclusion.

Humanity is on the verge of understanding that its childhood is ending, and we are here to support you in taking the first steps in your new life of adolescence. We encourage you to take responsibility for yourself and this world that you have inherited. In order for that to happen, the old paradigms will fall. They have to, for they were built on fear. In this New World, birthing itself through all of you, there will no longer be time or space for anything built on fear. The low frequency of fear cannot sustain itself in the new light of truth, peace and love now flooding this beautiful planet.

We ask you to choose love over fear in every moment. If you were able to do so, you would experience that which you call enlightenment or self-realisation. Most of you are not yet capable of making this fundamental shift and this is why we are speaking to humanity: to gift you with a spiritual guidance system that is as simple as it is profound. Yet we do not promise you a walk in a rose garden. Anyone promising freedom, peace and enlightenment in this manner does not speak the truth. There is no instant enlightenment! Rather, it is a long and delicate process to exchange fear for love and, as with every process, it takes time, especially in the third dimension. It will require your whole being to make this shift, and at times it will seem hard, but it is the only path offering you true freedom and inner peace, independent of all outer circumstances. You will learn to see through the eyes of love and recognise the Oneness of all beings.

Countless books have been written on spiritual matters and we are aware that this specific segment of the book market is extremely popular. What we see first and foremost in this phenomenon is that humanity is ready to ask questions and search for answers. This is the reason why we have waited for this particular time, when an adequate percentage of human consciousness has reached a higher vibration and is willing to receive our support.

We will offer you clarity in the jungle of spiritual teachings, truths and half-truths. Remember one thing: the truth is simple. Although truth may appear complex, it is always recognisable through its simplicity. This may guide you in your search, as will the following insight — listen to your heart and be aware of how it feels when you reflect on a teaching. Do you feel warm and more alive, with your heart expanding, even when presented with an inconvenient truth? Alternatively, do you feel uneasy or judged? On another occasion we will examine further the interesting subject of discernment. For now, we only wish to introduce ourselves and make our voice audible to the world.

We are very excited to come out from the invisible to speak to you and offer our service. A substantial part of humanity is ready for the embrace of truth. We are delighted to have the opportunity to plant the seeds of love in your consciousness, so that they may bear fruit a thousandfold, serving you in building the New World, no longer based on the old paradigm of fear and all her anxious children.

The New Earth is a place of love, truth and peace, and it is already emerging. We see this world already born and grown. It exists, we can assure you. We, who live beyond time and space, have watched the birth of our 'child', the New Earth. For you, this event may still appear in the imminent emerging future. It is only a matter of viewpoint and perspective, isn't it. Imagine, feel and dream the New World into existence, by choosing love over fear. Believe in your dreams of a better world and act accordingly. Only then can this world, already existing on a higher plane, manifest in your physical reality.

We want you to understand that *you* are birthing the New Earth into existence. Each one of you is called as a co-creator in making this New World of peace and love possible. For this to happen, become the conscious creator of your own life, learn about the original intended use of the mind and gain an understanding of the deeper meaning of your emotions, along with the ability to heal your pain. Comprehend the importance of detachment and reconsider your beliefs about who you are, what life means and why you are here.

We will lovingly assist you to leave the old world — the old 'you' — behind, for neither the old world, based on fear, nor your conditioned 'you' can be taken into the New World. Become love, peace and truth. Transform yourself, develop these virtues and once again discover that which you have always been since the beginning: truth, peace, love and light. You have never lost this light; it still lives within all of you. Few can remember or even believe that, beneath the thick layers of pain, fear and conditioning that cause you to live in a limited world, the light of Source is still shining. Even if its flame is tiny, it is still there, simply waiting to be reinvoked, to shine like a lighthouse and radiate love.

Dear ones, your light is no different from the light of a Master like Jesus or Buddha. The only difference is that they made space for this light under all circumstances. They served truth and love and so became an example for all of you to see the possibility of freedom and full awakening. Unfortunately, the religions established later used their lives to justify man-made laws and portrayed their spiritual achievements as being unattainable for the average person. This gave the impression that none of you could ever reach their heights. Jesus, Buddha, Isis, Mohammed, Krishna and Moses as with all Masters, known, unknown and long forgotten, came to the human race as your loving older brothers and sisters, to show you your own potential.

None of them wanted to be worshipped, nor would they have agreed to become the founders of world religions with all the rules, rites and laws built around their original teachings of truth. Sadly, at the same time the core essence of these sacred teachings was lost.

The establishment of religions has in actual fact totally missed the point. The enlightened Masters gave you the keys to true freedom, and religions turned these keys of freedom into prison walls. We do not judge this unfortunate unfolding of events, for a better outcome could not have been expected based on the level of consciousness of humanity and its leaders at that time. The dark ages have now passed and we wish to support you, along with other servants of the Light of the One, to rediscover the true teachings of the Masters, which have existed since eternity.

As humanity awakens, it will understand that enlightenment is not a luxury for the spiritual elite. It is your human birthright and the sole purpose of your existence. Everyone is called on this sacred journey. All of you who have deep desire, commitment, courage and love for truth are able to achieve freedom from ignorance along with inner peace and Oneness with the Divine. Welcome to this most exciting journey – your journey home!

3

CHANGE FROM WITHIN

We would like to describe how the average human life appears to us. We do not judge you with our observation; instead we wish to encourage you to widen your perspective of what is possible and support you on your search for the true meaning of life. Human beings often seem to take on inherited views from previous generations without questioning them on a broader scale. Some changes seem to be permitted and even expected; however, you do not dare to question the very foundations of these beliefs. This is exactly what we encourage you to do. Do not leave a stone unturned in relation to your beliefs about yourself as a human being, including your identity, health, illness, spirituality, life purpose, ageing, human potential, lifestyle, judgment of good and bad, the concept of death, divinity, enlightenment and so on.

You may consider these comments provocative, but from our point of view this is necessary, as we see humanity as being stuck in inherited and outdated beliefs. These concepts only support limitation, spiritual slumber and oblivion, preventing you from becoming a full expression of your unlimited divine consciousness. This is the true purpose of your life and the only cause worthy of our attention. We will not encourage you to stay on your old tracks, for this only leads to stagnation and has brought you to the point where you are now on the brink of a global suicide of apocalyptic dimensions.

We see you are at a major crossroad. We also see, for all of you, the opportunity to expand your consciousness and exchange your narrow beliefs for unlimited insights and ever-growing curiosity. This transformation will bring true life back to you and your starving world. You do not have to be clairvoyant or a genius to come to the conclusion that there is something fundamentally wrong with the way humanity is treating itself and this beautiful planet. The vast majority of today's population would agree with this simple statement. Let us lead you to the core of the answer to the question of why this has happened. We can only point to the first line of this book, where we said that it all began with humanity's disconnection from its divine origin or, to be precise, with your illusionary belief that you are separate from Source, which is in the sense of absolute reality impossible. The truth is that most human beings have lost their conscious connection with Source and therefore still firmly hold on to the concept of separation. This false assumption infiltrates everything you do, feel, think and act upon. It is like a dark undercurrent that sabotages the anchoring of your life in peace, love and truth.

We do not judge you for being caught up in this illusion, yet your false beliefs have potentially fatal consequences for humanity and the earth. We feel deep compassion, but from our viewpoint it is hard to believe that you hold on to this painful illusion, which is creating endless variations of limitation and fear. The situation can be compared with the well-known image of the bird living in a cage with its doors wide open. Although the little bird is free to leave, it is so used to its imprisonment that it never crosses the threshold. It never dares to taste freedom, nor does it ever dream of using its wings to fly. Sadly, this analogy reflects our observation of your present state of consciousness.

Dear ones, the prison doors are open wide and it is time that you realise this. You are the only ones holding yourselves back. You are free. Free to cross the threshold, free to fly! Free to try out your wings and test them to see if they will carry you into the unknown element of Spirit. You perceive yourself as creatures of the earth, but, we assure you, you are also inhabitants of the heavens. From the beginning you were meant to be the bridge between heaven and earth. Your body is born from this earth and your spirit descended from heaven. You were chosen to unite both energies within you, to bring the light of heaven to earth and the energies of earth up to the heavens. You were designed to be the living Yin–Yang, the embodiment and symbol of perfect balance, also described as the sacred alchemistic marriage. You are here to spiritualise matter and to materialise Spirit. This is your actual job description. You are here to become a unique expression of truth and to manifest your divine light. This is why, eons ago, we started the experiment of the human race.

We know most of you have forgotten this, and sense your scepticism in relation to what we are saying. It may sound like a fairytale or simply too nice to be true, and as a result you may not wish to entertain these ideas. We need to tell you, however, that now is the time for you to listen, to wake up from your dream of limitation and a life that is preoccupied with too many pointless activities and duties. You have forgotten the main purpose of why you came here, which is to understand the true nature of life, awaken and become a full expression of your divine self. You are divine. Your humanness is only an expression of your unlimited divine energy.

Humanity, rise from your deep slumber! Stop sleepwalking through life and finding safety in your self-constructed prison walls of limitation. Taste freedom and have the courage to remember this ancient truth that seems to appear so new.

There is no more time to waste. Time as you know has begun to collapse. Have you not recognised that time is speeding up? A year rushes by and it feels like only a few months have passed.

People of the earth, we want as many of you as possible to hear our call and listen with your hearts. The world as you know it is going to end. A New World is emerging that is more wonderful than anything you have ever dreamed of. Yet the New Earth is not coming to you entirely as a gift. It needs your full participation to be brought to life. This requires your total commitment to living in alignment with your soul and Higher Self, which communicate with you through your emotions, your heart and even your physical body. Do not ignore this sacred call any longer! Begin to understand that everything you are looking for in the outside world lies deep within your own innermost core.

In truth, there is no-one outside of you. Everything you see, together with how you perceive your surroundings, is simply a reflection of your inner aspects. All you see is you! Trees and flowers grow on the side of the street, other human beings come and go, but how you perceive them — your interpretation of it all — is entirely up to you. Everything you see is nothing but a reflection of your consciousness. The same event or person is perceived in a completely different manner by two people who may be viewing the scene from the same place and at the same time. Turn inwards, for nothing can be found on the outside. Realign your inner world and then the outside world will follow and reflect your inner harmony, beauty, love and peace. Your world is out of order because you are out of order! Or, as it is also said, what you perceive on the outside is only a reflection of what lies within.

Open your eyes, which have become used to blinding illusions, and begin to realise who you are and unearth your true nature. There is no-one else besides you who will save this world. You need to understand that, without your full commitment and cooperation, this change is impossible. You will birth the New Earth through your own being. Your shift in consciousness will parallel the ascension of Mother Earth, prophesied long ago. Although what we see on your planet is concerning, we are delighted to observe the tremendous will of the many who want to learn, know and remember.

Not only do you believe in limitation, inherited from previous generations, you also have little understanding of human emotions, the purpose of your mind and how to treat your physical body. Most of you have no idea of what spiritual alignment means, which is the main purpose of life. The majority of human beings are too busy with responsibilities and occupied with duties, career, raising children and paying their bills to even consider spiritual matters. This is why you put this important task on the back burner and label it as a luxury for times like holidays and retirement. You will not have the opportunity to do so for much longer. The frequency on this planet is increasing daily. Indecisiveness, spiritual slumber, unconsciousness, irresponsibility and ignorance will soon have imminent and inconvenient consequences. In fact, they have already begun.

Let us explain why this is so. It is due to the steady increase of higher energies descending on planet earth. It will soon be impossible to stay unconscious or blind towards your own inner conflicts, judgments and denial. Let us compare this situation with the analogy of the bright sun entering a dark room, lit by a single candle. In the soft candlelight the place appears cosy and clean. Yet, when the bright sunlight streams into the room, suddenly all the dust and junk that could not be seen before becomes visible. You feel uncomfortable and sense the urge to clean. This is exactly what is happening on earth. The bright light of the New Morning is engulfing all of you, making your pain and dysfunction visible.

We wish to invite you to begin your own inner clearing and healing process. We want you to understand yourself, your emotions, your mind, the needs of your physical body and, most important of all, your own divinity. No-one's inner light is better than the light of another. The only difference is that some of you make more space for the light than do others. It is the same light that enlightens all of us. From this place of Oneness, we embrace you and invite you on this sacred journey. Are you ready? We are!

4

YOU ARE NOT YOUR PHYSICAL BODY

When we look at humanity we observe that the physical body seems to be your sole identification. Most of you perceive your physical form as 'I', and because of this limited and false perception you fear death greatly, which is entirely unnecessary. You need to become aware that each and every one of you has personally chosen his time of leaving this embodiment. In fact, with this flawed belief in the reality of death, you deny the immortality of your soul. This narrow perception — believing you are your body — is causing unnecessary suffering that, besides creating a fear of death, is also fuelling the new beauty, anti-ageing and plastic surgery industries. These kinds of services would not and could not exist if humanity would correct this misguided understanding. Furthermore, this belief keeps you in the dark about the true meaning of death and therefore has far-reaching consequences.

You are not your body, but you have a physical form, which is the densest expression of your immortal being. You materialised your spirit into matter by creating this body, which is in itself a miracle. You as a soul did this with the help of many spiritual beings specialised in this sacred process and also with the support of your parents. You might have heard this before, but we want you to fully understand the difference between true comprehension, which means living in accordance with certain insights, or just 'believing' in something and not acting upon it. Do you see what we mean? As long as a belief just lingers at the periphery of your consciousness and is nothing but a verbal statement, this insight that you have a body, but you are not your body, will make little difference in your life or behaviour. Yet, when it becomes your truth, it will change your identification with limitation. But this will only be possible when you do your research with your heart and soul and discover the truth. Only personal experience will set you free.

We will question your perceptions about your physical body, because they are nothing but long-held beliefs in your collective unconscious and not solid facts, as you might assume. When we look at the fast-developing anti-ageing and plastic surgery industries, it makes us smile. You try to cure the symptoms without having found the cause! Accelerated ageing, which most of you are experiencing, is the result of ignorance as to how to treat your bodies the right way. What do we mean by 'bodies'? Besides the physical form, every human being has several other bodies, invisible to the human eye. Without them your body would die instantly. It is because of these finer bodies, dwelling in your physical form, that an aura is emanating from your body.

There are several layers of these invisible bodies, each having a different function. The first is the 'etheric body', which gives life force to your physical form. An experienced healer is able to observe disturbance in this energy field long before it manifests in the physical as an illness. Then there are the 'emotional body' and the 'mental body'. The emotional body is where all of your feelings originate. Unfortunately, this energy field is not an expression of harmony in most of you, because humans generally do not love themselves. From this root cause, which is just another illusion, stem most of the contradictory and self-destructive feelings that seriously affect your physical health.

You need to understand that all of these bodies affect one another and are not separate, even if you would like to think that way. Uncleared and unhealed negative emotions get trapped in the physical body and block the flow of the life force (chi, prana) in the etheric body, creating physical illness after a prolonged period of time and intensity. The same applies for negative thoughts. If you hold on to fear-based thoughts, repeat them often enough and add the compatible emotions, then the same process will automatically take its course. Negative thought forms can create illness and speed up the ageing process. It is unnecessary for ageing to occur the way you currently experience it in your world.

It is your ignorance about how to treat all of your bodies that is causing preventable illness and early ageing. With the correct education regarding your emotions, mind, life force and spiritual alignment from the moment you were born, you would not experience sickness and premature ageing to the extent you do today. There would be no fear of the transition you call death, because you would truly understand this sacred event and not be left guessing, contemplating with both hope and fear a process that is natural and unavoidable. Some of you would even gain mastership over all your bodies and live in full alignment with your Higher Self. In this way they could demonstrate their mastery to the rest of you by leaving their physical form consciously and willingly, without fear, whenever they chose to do so. This would be very different from the way it is today, where your physical vehicle can become so sickness-ridden that it is completely unusable.

Can you feel the sense of freedom when we talk about the most feared subject on your planet — death? Our perception of death is very different. For us it is a reason for welcoming you home and celebrating all of your achievements and experiences on earth. We will focus more on the subject of death at a later time, to give it the full attention it deserves.

You have now learned that the mental, emotional and etheric bodies are influencing your physical form, depending on how wisely you use and treat them. There is another body, which consists of many different layers, but for the sake of simplicity and better understanding we would like to give them all just one name — 'the spiritual body'. Sadly, most human beings are disconnected from this body and hold only an unconscious connection to it. This is in fact a catastrophe. It can be considered the primary cause of all wars, violence, injustice and disasters, including every illness on earth. You have forgotten that you are spiritual beings who are here to have a human experience and not, as most of you believe, that you are human beings who might, if you search for long enough and try hard enough, have a spiritual experience.

Understand the gravity of this statement, for this assertion alone can change the way you perceive life. You will then truly comprehend that you have completely disconnected from your divine origin.

You replaced your spiritual heart with your mind. Originally, your heart was the portal to your Higher Self and the guidance for your mind. Now the mind tries desperately to make sense of the complexities of life, its challenges and contradictions. Yet the mind was never meant to give you this direction. Its initial purpose was to serve your Higher Self and to be instructed with the wisdom and guidance from your sacred heart.

This true knowledge seems to be long forgotten, for you have collectively reached a point where you are solely identified with your physical form and your mind is running your life. If you are spiritually interested, you might study the colours of the aura field or read about the existence of the Higher Self, but for most of you these finer subtle realities remain only abstract concepts. As a result, many seekers end up giving their power away to priests, monks, religions, churches, guides and spiritual teachers who claim to have a more direct connection to the light.

We have said that we will shake the foundations of your belief systems. We have to, because most of your concepts are built on fear and ignorance. They have only one purpose, which is to keep you separate from Source, separate from who you truly are. You therefore crave power. But all you will find is worldly power, which can never satisfy the hunger of your soul. Only true power can fulfil this sacred longing. True power comes from the complete merging with your Higher Self. Then, freedom, peace and unconditional love will be found.

You need to become more interested in the truth regarding how to correctly treat your physical body, your emotions and your mind, along with the alignment with your divine light. There is no other way! Star ships are here, but not to save the chosen few, as some apocalyptic cults might have you believe. Earth and humanity have never had the level of support that you have now, where almost the entire universe is watching your first steps into self-responsibility and spiritual maturity. In healing your emotions, gaining a better understanding of the mastery of your mind and nurturing your physical body with a diet containing life force by avoiding dead and highly processed food, your fear of ageing will greatly diminish. Botox and plastic surgery will become a thing of the past and you will look back at these times of confusion in utter disbelief, with the understanding that it was due to ignorance. You simply did not learn how to live in harmony with yourself and reflect your divinity.

Everything in the universe functions in line with the oldest symbol on earth: the Spiral. All is created from the inside out and never the other way around. Altering outer appearance or manifestation will never correct the errors and imbalances created on the inner and finer level of vibration, which functions like a blueprint. Only when you change this blueprint by addressing the true cause of illness and ageing will you be able to find the cure. We encourage you to study the true purpose of life.

We, who have appeared in many forms and under many names in the past as the Masters, as you call us today, or the Enlightened Ones, again want to make it clear that we came to encourage *all of you* to follow our footsteps and claim mastery over yourselves. Then you will be welcomed home and claim your rightful place as one of 'the Children of the Sun', who serve the One.

5

WE ARE THE HEART OF GOD

You might find it unusual, even unthinkable, to comprehend that your Creator is speaking to you. Your established belief systems generally assume that this direct contact is impossible for the people of today, having been reserved only for the prophets of the past. We would like to correct this error in thinking and assure you that everyone is able to connect with God — the Goddess — your Creator — Source — the Divine. You are all a part of us and we are a part of you.

So how can it be that you believe direct contact to the Divine is the privilege of a chosen few? Again, this is nothing but a limited belief put in place by organised religions, lost in outer rituals and laws and completely missing the point of the sacred teachings of truth. As a result of this disconnection from your higher power, you misunderstood almost all that we gave to guide you to true freedom. All religions that are not built on truth will fall. You might be shocked to hear this, but nevertheless it is the truth.

Again you might ask: Who is talking here and proclaiming they are the Source of all Life — the Heart of God? We know that you have not yet fully understood who is talking to you, so we would like to further clarify our identity, even though we are aware that our answer might cause more confusion for some, because it will further stretch your concepts and beliefs. This is exactly what we want! We need to provoke you to recognise the truth. Again, who are we? We said that we are the Heart of God, we are the Source of all Life, we are the Nameless One, we are your Creator and we are Love.

What does this mean? We are the unlimited field of consciousness from where everything was born, including all Masters like Buddha, Jesus, Mohammed, Krishna, Moses. They are all expressions of the One, and only different appearances of All That Is. All That Is is all that exists. All That Is is talking to you — talking to you directly. Even if you doubt this, it is nevertheless exactly what is occurring: God the Creator itself is speaking to all of humanity in human language. You might not believe that this is possible, but it is happening here right now, in front of you, to prove you wrong. We decided it is time to contact humanity directly and chose English, a language spoken by a vast majority, to share our message with the world.

You may now be thinking, wait a moment, did you just say God is speaking to us and that God, from whom descended Jesus, Buddha, Mohammed, Krishna and Moses, says that there was only one consciousness birthing all of these holy men? And that they are all only different expressions of one divine consciousness? That is right — this is exactly what we are saying. This is also true for all other Masters known, unknown and long forgotten. We have always come to you in different forms and disguises and in varying circumstances. Yet we were always the same I AM THAT I AM.

It follows that all disputes throughout history over which of your religions was right were entirely pointless. It is like saying that one part of God believes that it is superior to another, which is ridiculous. We understand that from your level of deep separation consciousness you were unable to see the face of the One in other spiritual teachings. You could only recognise the truth in the teaching you chose to call your own. When humanity is ready to embrace the consequences of this statement, your world will make a giant leap towards unity consciousness. So when we say 'we', you know now that the consciousness that birthed Buddha, Krishna, Moses, Jesus, Mohammed and all other Masters is talking in Oneness and unity to you.

We are aware that this is not easy to accept. This announcement goes against all of your established beliefs, but, as you know by now, we do not hold your limited beliefs in high regard, for we recognise the pain and fear they have created. It is our love and care for your soul that leads us to provoke you and if necessary destroy what does not ring true. This is what you call 'tough love'. We believe that now is the time for tough love for humanity. You will be unable to step in to an expanded consciousness and higher vibration if everything remains the same. In actual fact, we wish to make you aware that nothing will stay the same.

This is why we decided to contact you, as you are already well into the preparation for the greatest shift of consciousness humanity has experienced. Although there are countless books written about this change, the majority of you still do not understand what this transformation really means. Some of you might expect big catastrophes, but is your world not already a catastrophe?

Please take a look. What have you done to this planet and to one another? It seems you do not care. You do not love yourself, which is why you cannot love each other. You still believe in war as a legitimate option for resolving conflict. Furthermore, it is of concern that most of you can live with the fact that those of you in the developed countries have more than enough, sometimes too much, whereas over a third of humanity, who are your brothers and sisters, do not even have sufficient to eat, let alone clean water, medical care, education and basic human rights.

If you loved yourself and had opened your heart, which is your sacred connection to your Higher Self — your 'phone line' to God — you would no longer tolerate this injustice and would do something about it. Within a short period of time you would find solutions for this inequality, change the horrendous living conditions and be more interested in helping one another to create a better, fairer and loving world.

Your indifference towards the unfairness between the first and third worlds is only one aspect of our concern. We want you to look at how you treat the earth, your Mother, which is what the ancient tribes have called her forever. Do you really believe that you can survive when you continue to disregard and exploit the very foundation of your living and survival? We think you all know the answer. But who is acting? The list of instances of abuse of human rights and of the environment is endless. Your world is a catastrophe — and we mean, along with *your* world, *you* as creators of this world. What are you waiting for?

Our call goes out to all of humanity to change and get involved. You need to realise that you are all connected; you are all one. If one country is suffering, the rest of the world feels its impact. If one country is starving, if one country has bent the laws of justice, you are all influenced by this tragedy. You are all called to correct the errors and imbalances in order to create a better future. At the same time, as you extend your helping hand to your fellow man, you need to heal yourself and come into alignment with your true nature. Only then will the world heal; only then will you all be able to move into the higher vibration of the New Earth.

Do you now understand why nothing can remain the same? Nothing will stay the same, neither you nor your world. All has to adjust to the higher frequencies now enveloping this planet. What an exciting time to witness the greatest shift of consciousness humanity has ever experienced! Have courage and remember your heart. There is great help at hand.

6

HEALING

Did you know or even consider as a possibility that you can totally reinvent yourself? The human body rebuilds itself continuously. In fact, every seven years you have a completely new body. Unfortunately, most of you unconsciously re-create your physical body in a way that it looks and functions the same as before. You do not use this incredible opportunity to modify the cellular information and, as a result, the cells rebuild themselves based on the old memory provided by the DNA. Unless you deliberately reprogram these data, your body consciousness will always reproduce the same cell structure as before.

You may wish to pause for a moment and allow what we have said to digest. Yes, we indeed said that you can reprogram your DNA by providing different information to your cells — another blueprint so to speak — and the cells will rebuild themselves according to these new data. This sounds exciting, and without a doubt it is. So how can you do that? Consciousness is the key, and not genetic engineering — which appears to be a rather primitive form of healing when one understands the true secrets of consciousness.

So allow us now to assist in familiarising you with this new concept. We will explain how you can influence and alter the genetic information stored in the DNA, as your third-dimensional thinking does not allow for such possibilities at the moment. Was it not one of your greatest physicists, Albert Einstein, who said that everything is energy? This is the way we perceive reality. Consequently, your physical body, with all of its cells, also has to be energy. Therefore, all small particles of each cell must be energy, which includes its information centre, the DNA. We have just mentioned the possibility of influencing and changing your DNA information with consciousness, but what is consciousness? Is it not energy as well? Now it no longer seems an impossibility to change your DNA, which is energy, with consciousness, which is also energy.

In order for this to happen, several things need to occur simultaneously. First, you need to connect with your Higher Self, which is one with Source, the highest energy in creation. Through this connection you access the purest essence of Love — the Divine, the ultimate omnipotent power — which has created everything. Healings described in the Bible and other sacred scripts only occurred because Christ or another advanced healer tapped into the unlimited field of Source and fully understood that he was one with the Divine. Thus, there was no longer any difference between the human and the Divine. He realised his own divinity and the creator force became available for his use, and so he fulfilled the deeper meaning of the word human (hu = divine, man = man, human = divine man). This, too, is your destiny: to become truly human, a divine man. When you are in alignment with your creator force, you bring healing, love, peace and harmony into your physical world.

Let us return to where we began, with the story of the healer who created miracles. From our viewpoint, miracles do not exist. So-called miracles are simply the precise use of higher spiritual knowledge. The healer tapped into the unlimited field of creation, and this high energy was transformed through his hands and heart and flowed into the body of someone in need. What happened in this process? Source energy, which is pure love, was conveyed to a body in disharmony or disease (dis-ease), and it brought order, balance and harmony into the cellular structure, along with healthy new information to the DNA.

Some healers directed the divine force with intention, whereas others allowed the light to do the healing work. What truly mattered was the purity of consciousness and heart of the healer and his ability to align with Source, without interference from his human nature.

To become a pure channel for the Divine is not an easy task, and preparation for it involves a lifetime, sometimes even several lifetimes, of training. It is possible, as we have demonstrated on many occasions. We simply wanted to show, with this explanation of healing, that what you label as a miracle is only an event outside of your common belief system.

You need to understand that this form of healing is the result of the alignment with divine will and the precise use of higher knowledge, attained through the thorough study of spiritual science. This can be achieved by every soul who is willing to go through the tough training. Would you call it a miracle when a rocket flies to the moon? You would have some decades ago, but since humanity took this step this is no longer called a miracle; instead it is understood to be the fruit of scientific endeavour. In the near future, what you call unexplained healings will be seen as the correct use of higher knowledge and divine power.

Since the beginning, the use of the 'Power of the Light' was taught in the Sacred Mystery Schools. Students went through intensive spiritual training until all of their bodies were cleansed, in full alignment with Source, and so prepared to use this sacred energy. We want to explain why this thorough training was necessary. As previously mentioned, the calling of a soul to align with Source generally took many lifetimes of preparation in order to become an embodiment of the Higher Self and live as its expression on earth. This was the only way we could ensure that the student would not abuse this power, harm himself or others or even cause destruction with this sacred energy. You need to comprehend that energy is in itself neutral and the intent of the disciple determines the quality of its use. It is thus not only important to align to Source, live in harmony, cleanse and heal yourself, it is also about purity of heart to ensure the correct use of power. You may ask why we are telling you stories from a long-forgotten past. We use these examples to demonstrate that the all-too-common impatience of spiritual seekers is dangerous and can potentially have far-reaching negative consequences for their own inner development as well as for others.

Please understand there is no instant enlightenment, even when some of you would like to believe that sitting at the feet of a spiritual teacher for long enough will do the job for you. We assure you, it will not. No-one can do the job for you. You have to walk your own path every step of the way. Do not give your power away. Never fall prey to the illusion that there is someone embodying an aspect that is not also within you. You may not yet have fully developed these abilities, but you would not be able to recognise them in others if you did not carry these seeds yourself. Remember, there is nothing outside of you. All you see is a reflection of yourself. This applies to the positive as well as the negative attributes you observe in others.

So open your eyes and truly begin to see. Take your power back if you have given it away to a teacher, healer, therapist, partner, friend, saint or guru. Christ, Buddha and all the Enlightened Ones do not need your power. We are the Force. You need your power in order to grow, reach your goals and follow your heart's desire. That is why God gave you this power. It is not meant to be given to others. It is the horse that rides you through the storm of life — and, we assure you, you will need it.

Dear ones, our true teachings have been significantly altered and misinterpreted throughout the course of history. Sometimes our teachings were even turned into the opposite. It is time to set the record straight. Understand that every inner development process takes time to fully settle into your whole being. You cannot achieve self-realisation through attending a few workshops, bathing in the light of a teacher and leaving with the conviction that you have awakened because you had a mystical experience. Your everyday life is your spiritual teacher. Life encourages you to open up your heart to your soul, to decipher the hidden messages behind the daily events. It is always the hand of the Divine providing you with what you need. Always.

When an inconvenient situation arises, remember it is the Divine sending you a message. Begin to see with our eyes, God's eyes, with the eyes of Christ and Buddha, and your life will change dramatically. You will enter the real world, contrary to the world you call real at the moment, which in truth is nothing but an illusion. You will become a member of the 'Sacred Mystery School of the Heart'. Slowly your inner eyes will open to truth, peace will enter your soul and you will only feel love.

We do not intend to call humanity to walk with us for much longer. We are walking, and whoever wishes to join us may join us. For those who choose to remain too busy with life's entanglements, so it will be. Listen, humanity: it is time to decide. Know your decision will have consequences. This is not meant as a threat — it is the truth. Never before have you seen or lived through anything of the magnitude that is about to unfold. This shift will change life forever on planet earth. Prepare yourself by aligning to your true nature, by clearing your bodies and by healing your negative emotions and thoughts. Leave the rest up to the Divine. You need to understand that there are only two directions. You either walk on the road to freedom and love or you remain stuck where you are. There is nothing in between. Welcome to the most exciting time in human history.

7

LOVE

Let us talk about love. You use this word a lot. It seems to be everywhere — written on T-shirts and bags, and most of your stories, songs and movies circle around the topic of love. Humanity appears to be obsessed with love, or at least with the word. It seems to us that you are preoccupied with this subject because you are trying to find its true meaning.

Although your world is filled with the word love, you do not yet understand love. If you did truly comprehend the meaning of love there would be no need to dwell on it — you would simply *be* love. This is it — to be love! Yet how can you BE love? From our perspective, you are looking for love in all the wrong places. Love can only be found within the innermost core of your own being, which is love itself. From this foundation you will be able to love yourself and others.

Remember what we said about the Spiral, the oldest symbol on earth — our symbol, the symbol of Source, the symbol of the Great Mother, the symbol of Creation. Everything develops from the inside out. Have a look at nature: there is first a seed, then a sprout, a fragile plant, a little bud, a beautiful flower, a fruit, a seed, and so the process begins again. This is the sacred cycle of life. The whole wisdom of creation is laid out in front of your eyes, but who bends his knees to honour the Divine's revelation?

Everywhere you look in creation you will find the same principle, and this also applies to you and your search for love. You can only find love deep within your own heart and soul. You are the very love that you are looking for in your outer world.

In truth, your desperate search for the right partner is your deepest longing for your own true nature. When you fully comprehend this statement, you will take the first step in breaking free from one of the biggest illusions of humanity — the quest for the perfect mate. There is no such thing as 'the perfect mate'. This is nothing but a romantic concept created by your longing and inner incompletion. You first need to become your own best friend, the perfect mate for yourself, and then your vibration of completion will attract another human being with a similar level of inner achievement and you will live together in harmony, love and respect.

This relationship you have with yourself has two important aspects. First is the alignment to your Higher Self and second is the connection to your human aspect, where it is required that you become your own best friend. For this to happen, you need to heal, understand, love and accept all of your imperfections as well as encourage, support and respect yourself. Only then, from the platform of this stable inner foundation, can a loving relationship develop with another person. Generally you try to do it the other way around. You do not love yourself, you have no conscious connection to your Higher Self, and from this position of lack you look desperately for someone out there to protect you, love all of you, love the aspects you cannot love about yourself and make you feel safe. In this respect, humanity is collectively caught in a cosy but childish dream that does not work. Look at your divorce rate and the number of heartbreaks — love is written about everywhere, yet so rarely found.

We are placing the ancient symbol of the Spiral, this powerful energetic sign, on to planet earth to correct your errors of perception. We will lay the sacred Spiral over all of your concepts regarding your external search for love, because you need to understand that nothing but the reflections from within can be found in the outer world. When your inner life is unfulfilled and fearful, how can there be space for true love? Under these conditions you will only attract people who reflect your incompletion and, despite your desperate search, you will again be left feeling empty and lonely. Why not try the other path? Close your eyes to the outer world for a while and direct your focus towards your unknown inner world, where all treasures you could ever dream of can be found. To turn inwards costs nothing but your honest effort — and it is the same effort for everyone, whether young or old, rich or poor, male or female and so on. Only in the darkness of your unknown can you find the love you are all looking to find on the outside.

We see how much effort you put into being loved — being someone important, someone loveable. In fact, most of your achievements in life are attained to prove to yourself that you are good enough and loveable. Titles, money, career, possessions, beautiful partner and so on — all just to validate that you are worthy of love. You would not have to go through all of this if you knew the secrets of your heart. Unveil the mystery of your existence by turning inwards, into the sacred land of your soul. Holy books and spiritual teachings from all nations and the wisdom of the ancient tribes talk in their essence of this inner journey, but who among you has listened? For many thousands of years the secrets have been written on the sacred walls of your heart, but few have journeyed there to decipher their meaning.

The time is coming to an end where people ridicule those following the call of their soul and living life in integrity. Times are changing. In the future, those who do not listen will be considered foolish, for their choices will be seen as ignorant, causing only trouble and disharmony. What we are teaching will become common knowledge for all inhabitants on earth. Everyone will be called to take responsibility for himself.

Let us turn our focus back to love. What does love mean? Does it mean I do everything for someone I love or that I give my power away to someone I love? Does it mean that I forget about my own dreams and begin to dream the dreams of someone I love? Does it mean that I am willing to suffer to the extreme, only to be with someone I believe I love? Does it mean I tolerate injustice, violence, verbal, emotional and physical abuse because I am convinced that the extent of suffering I am able to endure equals the depth of love I feel for someone?

We think that we have now given sufficient examples of possible beliefs about love to show that what most of you have experienced or are experiencing cannot be love. But most of you have at one time been entangled in unhealthy relationships and some of you still are. This fact only demonstrates the extent of your separation from your true nature. We cannot emphasise enough that the only way to stop this unnecessary pain is to turn inwards and first establish a relationship with yourself. You need to become your own best friend and begin the inner journey towards your True Self. Love that has earned the name love radiates from the inside out. Only when you unconditionally love yourself are you able to love others. Then the Divine — the purest love — will shine from your heart and enlighten the world. Yet, Love never pleases. Love always gives what you need. Love is wise and has all-seeing eyes. Love is tender. Love can be tough. Love simply *is*. Love has created everything and Love sustains all. Love is what IS. Love is you. Love is us. Love is All That Is.

Love does not need. Feel the aspects in you that are still in need and take them to your heart. The majority of you avoid pain, for you have not yet learned how to love your unhealed parts. No-one will love these aspects for you — you have to learn to love your own wounds. Each time you find yourself reacting, hurting, jealous, needy, angry or greedy, literally take this aspect into your arms and bring it to your heart. Love this part like a mother comforting her suffering child. Then call the Divine to heal this abandoned part by enveloping it with white-golden light. All of you are able to do this small but profound exercise, which will change your life for the better and lead you to greater inner freedom.

You are all searching for one thing, and that is love. Do you know that you can only receive what you first give to yourself or are willing to give to others? This is one of the universal laws. Are you ready to act in greater alignment with the wisdom of the ages, reflected in these laws? The sacred knowledge and truth recorded in the ancient scripts has never changed, but few have listened. Now humanity is at a major crossroad and you can no longer afford not to listen. It is now time for you to act!

8

As It Is Above So It Is Below

We would like to examine the divine law 'As it is above, so it is below'. This also has its reflection as 'What you perceive in your outer world is a mirror image of your inner world'. This law is like a living hologram. When you begin to explore this sacred principle, at first it appears to be two-dimensional, but in truth this law reflects a multidimensional reality and is alive — as with all universal laws. These sacred laws are expressions of the living breath of God.

On earth, your laws seem to be abstract concepts written on paper, without fire and without life. Yet this is not how creation functions and only shows that your approach is out of alignment with the true forces of life. This is the reason why a judge on earth is required to undertake such a lengthy education and adjudicating complex legal matters is a time-consuming process. This would be unnecessary if you were connected to your sacred heart and thus linked to the Divine. You would swiftly gain insights of wisdom in judging a situation or a person and their circumstances from a point of higher knowing. A verdict gained in this manner would provide everyone involved with an opportunity for inner growth and the appropriate support to correct the mistaken beliefs that have led to their erroneous deeds.

This is the direction your justice system will take in the New World. Society will assist people who have made these errors in judgment in order to correct their behaviour. Furthermore, you will support these individuals to heal their wounds, which were the true cause of their harmful actions, thus allowing harmony to return to their lives. On the New Earth you will witness the disappearance of judgment, condemnation and crime. In the transition phase, crime will be understood as an outcry of the soul that has lost its inner centre and is disconnected from its true nature. With this new understanding you will be unable to maintain a position of blame and judgment. Your hearts will go out to these people, who did not receive enough loving support in their earlier years. Do you realise this is what Jesus meant when he said: Love your enemies? It is hurt people who hurt people. When you fully comprehend the true meaning of this sentence, your perception of others will significantly change and the primal urge to judge will finally cease.

It is all about balance. When someone is out of balance, which means out of alignment with his True Self, disharmony will occur on the outside, even to the extreme where one takes the life of another. Your future society will put its main focus on the prevention of crime by supporting and educating parents in the art of raising their children in a respectful, harmonious and balanced way. Parents who are unbalanced will be supported to heal and grow. As we know already, all change needs to come from the inside out. In the higher dimensions we are interested in examining the cause of problems, and it makes little sense to us to battle against symptoms.

The way you treat individuals who are out of balance and cause harm to society is ineffective and an utter waste of time. The treatment of your fellow humans through judgment, singling them out in society and not supporting their inner healing will only cause further harm in the future. The motivation behind these kinds of actions stems from fear, which is why the efficiency of your prison system is questionable. In the truest sense its failure is highlighted by the large numbers of re-offenders. Your legal system is based on fear, and it is not working. Only a method founded on love, true insight, healing and the firm will to help your brothers and sisters to reintegrate into society will have long-term success.

You may get the impression that we are relentless critics, but this is not intended. Our wish is to transmit insights into the different layers and functions of society to reveal their energetic origin — fear or love — to enable you to judge why some methods are working and others are not. Everything born from fear will simply create further fear — it will never heal or enable you to establish a stable, healthy and harmonious society. You need to look at everything with your inner eyes and study the science of truth. Learn to see with God's eyes and you will find solutions for all problems faster than you ever thought possible.

Examine the energetic pattern that founded your governments, your justice, your school and health systems, the institution of marriage and so on. Look at everything of importance in your life, study its energetic origin and ask the question: Is this organisation in alignment with the divine principles or is its underlying motivation fear?

Children of the earth, we are not joking when we tell you that everything will change and the world as you know it will cease to exist. All ruling, directing and governing institutions on this planet that have their energetic origin based in fear cannot be taken into the New World. Anything — and we mean anything — birthed from fear cannot make this sacred transition. It is energetically impossible for the high frequency of love to be compatible with the low frequency of fear.

We began this conversation with 'As it is above, so it is below' or, as it is sometimes put, 'That which you perceive in your outer world is only a reflection of what lies within'. We used the example of your behaviour towards criminals to demonstrate how this universal law applies. This law works in the vast universe as it does in your outer and inner worlds. In your external world you single people out who do not comply with the established laws, and punish, judge and abandon them. Not many of you are able to truly forgive a person who has failed and offer them a second chance. The majority of you label and brand them as criminals forever. This behaviour is born from ignorance and only reflects the way you treat your own imperfections, the parts of you that cannot keep up with the unrealistically high expectations you place on yourself.

It has taken us a while to guide you to this point. Nevertheless, we felt it was necessary to spend sufficient time on your conduct towards criminals to demonstrate that this behaviour is only a reflection of how you treat your own unloved parts. How can it be any different? Did we not say that the external world is nothing but a reflection of your inner world or, put in different terms, everything you allow others to do to you, you first do to yourself. It is also said: You treat others the same way that you treat yourself. Please let these principles of truth sink in and contemplate them.

Most of the pain humanity is suffering could be avoided if you would understand the full meaning of this truth. Let us again use the example of how you treat criminals. We believe that every individual with a certain degree of common sense would be aware that someone who has committed a crime is unbalanced and most likely did not have a stable, loving and supportive upbringing. Unfortunately, despite this realisation, you still judge, abandon and demonise these fellow human beings. We need to make you aware that you act exactly the same way towards your own wounded aspects. These are the parts that you dislike and feel ashamed off.

Most of you judge yourselves harshly and simply abandon these aspects. These unhealed parts feel unable to fulfil your unrealistic expectations of achieving perfection, and you sentence them — the secret messengers of your soul — into your inner dungeon. There they rot and from time to time cause inner riots, sabotaging your life with depression, drug addiction, eating disorders, alcohol abuse, sex addiction and various forms of illness. Their actual purpose, however, is to remind you that you are not this perfect person you would like to present to the world or even to yourself. You are human, and you need to understand and learn to love these unloved parts.

There is no other way. Look at your world. You have in the developed countries an explosive rise of depression, cancer and heart disease, all of which are connected to what we have just discussed. These illnesses are mainly caused by suppressed emotions stored in the body system, and there they create severe imbalance. Repression of emotions will lead to disease on a physical level if it has sufficient intensity and lasts long enough. Negative emotions do not just go away; they are either released through expression or stored in your bodies. In fact, psychologists, scientists and medical doctors are now discovering the connection between emotions and physical illness. Trapped emotions are slowly being recognised as major contributing factors for disease.

We believe that, in order to find the cure for the major causes of death in the developed countries, you need to comprehend that there is no other way but to learn the science of love and to rediscover the true meaning of human emotions and how to deal with them in a healthy manner. Only if you turn away from your well-known path of condemnation, judgment and the refusal to forgive will you cross the threshold of the New World. On the New Earth, all inhabitants will be trained in the art of love and so find the cures for the medical curses that plague the twenty-first century: depression, cancer and heart disease.

We are here to guide you, and we will provide further information in time when we see that you are acting upon our basic message. Then we will explain more advanced spiritual healing techniques. Sometimes when we look at humanity it appears to us that you behave in a way similar to a stubborn teenager who refuses to accept the insights of his parents. While this is the nature of being a teenager, you are in a dangerous phase where you are about to destroy yourselves, and this is the reason why we are stepping in, as any loving parent would. Reflect on what you have received and understand that we are acting out of love. You may compare us to your parents — in fact this parallel is much closer to the truth than you may believe.

9

YOU DO NOT LOVE YOURSELF

We would like to continue on our train of thought regarding your relationship with yourself and how you treat your wounded aspects. We consider the fact that the vast majority of humans do not love themselves as one of the root causes of all conflict and existing problems on earth. Without an acknowledgment of this concerning issue, there can be no cure for any of your problems, and you will remain unable to find satisfying solutions with lasting effects. This attitude towards yourself has energetically infected your collective emotional field like a cancer.

As we have previously stated, most of you believe that you are single identities, separate from each other. This is an impossibility and an utter illusion, but you are used to perceiving life along these lines. In truth you are all linked to each other, and everything that you do, think and feel is affecting the whole of humanity. We know some of you have heard this before, but see that the majority have not yet fully understood this fact.

Allow us to explain. Imagine someone is feeding the vast morphogenetic field, where humanity's collective thought forms and emotions are vibrating. Let us assume that this person is loving, so the energy being contributed to this field is positive and filled with love, understanding and peace. We could also say that this person's input is positive and enlightening and therefore accelerating the frequency of the whole field, and as a result everyone is benefiting. Although the majority of you are unaware of its direct impact, this does not diminish its effect.

Now let us consider someone who is expressing unconscious pain, hatred, anger and self-sabotage. These kinds of emotions stem from fear and are therefore vibrating on a lower frequency; the colours in the aura field of this person appear darkened and cluttered. These negative energies are also feeding the field but with the exact opposite effect. In one way or another all human beings unknowingly contribute to the morphogenetic field every second of their lives. You can decide whether you contribute more love and light or offer a negative vibration. The light you add will always lift and enlighten others, whereas the negativity you feed into the field will have the reverse effect.

Let us return our focus to where we began this conversation — to the statement that most members of the human race do not love themselves. Billions of people are therefore tapping into the morphogenetic field and feeding it with confirming negative thoughts and emotions. On a subconscious level, they are all convinced that they are not good enough and not loveable. So what happens when billions of people are continuously repeating this behaviour from generation to generation? The answer is simple: What they believe will become reality. This is how you create reality. Yet your definition of reality is very different from ours, for we define reality in the sense of absolute reality.

The way you use the term reality refers only to the accumulation of confirming thoughts and convictions. If enough people strongly hold the same belief for a lengthy period of time, then the consequence of this process will be that it appears to you as real. In time this belief is no longer questioned and is stated as fact, and eventually it becomes so-called reality and influences you on a daily basis. In truth, it simply means that enough people intensely believed in the same limitation for long enough. We mentioned earlier that we will shake the very foundation of how you perceive the world, and we believe it may slowly begin to make sense as to why this is necessary.

From now on you might be more cautious when accepting anything as a fact simply because a majority of people hold a particular belief, for this in itself does not mean much. Billions of you do not love yourselves and unfortunately remain unaware of this horrendous attitude, hidden in your subconscious. Nevertheless this belief acts as a powerful poison towards yourself and others. All children born are entering the field and absorbing this destructive information, like a mother's milk, into their own aura field and then acting accordingly. Throughout history, this is what has happened from generation to generation. It is now time to stop the chain reaction of handing this poisonous inheritance to your children. You are the first generation that has the opportunity, the knowledge and the tools to heal this enormous wound in the human psyche as a whole.

When you learn to love your imperfections, you will end this chain reaction of self-destruction and your future generations can grow up unburdened by its heavy load. Your actions constantly affect everyone else, for the better as well as for the worse, because you are all One. If you were to acknowledge this truth, you would realise that you are all cells in the great body of God, as are those you call Masters or the Enlightened Ones. The only difference between us, is that we know we are One and divine, whereas you have not yet come to this realisation. This is the reason why we remind you of what you forgot when passing through the veil of oblivion as you entered the physical plane.

Dear ones, there is no way around learning to love yourself with all of your imperfections. These abandoned aspects are causing havoc and illness in your world to remind you that your actions are unwise. Most of you identify with the well-built mask of an artificially created persona, but behind this mask you are trying to hide your vulnerability and inability to fulfil the unrealistically high expectations of society and yourself. These split-off parts scream to you through depression, cancer, heart attack and countless other forms of disease, begging to finally be heard. They speak the truth — they are the tears you never cried, the cries you never screamed, the desperation and worry you had to swallow. Love these aspects, listen to them, for this is the only way to integrate them and make you whole.

As you do, everyone around you will feel lighter, for you feed the field with love through your actions, thoughts and emotions. You will become a living example of healing through leading a truthful life, which will inspire and encourage others to embark on their own inner journey. Everything you do, you do for yourself *and* your brothers and sisters. We are all One and we are all love. You are all so deeply loved. Learn to love yourself and contribute to the Revolution of Love that is sweeping the planet. This is indeed what is happening: The Revolution of Love has begun. Come with us and love yourself — then you can truly love one another.

10

THE CORE OF ALL TEACHINGS

Is it not written in your holy scriptures that Jesus, who embodied the love aspect of the Divine, will come back 'as a thief in the night'? The time of 'The Reappearance of the Christ' is now! We are true to our promise, but our coming is not in the way that you might expect. Our Spirit is returning to earth in so many different ways, but still we stand as One to reveal the truth of the eternal teachings. We want to shout from the rooftops, in your churches, temples and mosques: 'Mohammed, Jesus, Moses, Krishna and Buddha are One,

one and the same consciousness who have taken on different appearances to express the many faces of the Divine here on earth.'

Yet we are not returning dressed in white robes with long beards to sit on the thrones that most religions have built for us. We will destroy your man-made thrones and concepts, not out of anger but from a place of love. Children of the earth, you need to undo that which does not serve your true wellbeing and the wellbeing of your planet. The established religions have largely created separateness instead of Oneness, which is the core of all true spiritual teachings. Again, we need to place the Spiral of Truth on all religious institutions, to restore the heart of our teachings, which tell the same ancient truth:

1. There is one Supreme Consciousness you may call God, Allah, the Great Void, the Universal Mother, the Absolute or simply Love, where all of creation comes from.
2. Humanity is one being.
3. Truth, love, peace and true power can only be found within.
4. Align with your Higher Self and become the true expression of your divine nature, which is love, peace and truth.
5. Do unto others as you would have them do unto you.
6. Freedom is your eternal birthright.
7. Do not project your unloved parts onto your brothers and sisters and thus create enemies.
8. You are all equal, and cells within the body of God.
9. Love is who you are.
10. There is nothing to fear. There is only love. Therefore choose love over fear.

These are the core principles of all spiritual teachings. Can you tell us what your temple rules and church laws have in common with these eternal truths? We taught you long ago that your temple is inside. We are not inventing the wheel anew, nor do we intend to present you with new teachings. Our wish is to free the spiritual teachings of today from the misinterpretations that have led millions down the wrong path. Do you realise that, if a religion is telling you that you are superior to someone else when you follow its rules, these teachings cannot come from Oneness — from God? A statement such as this is against the fundamental divine principle of Oneness.

Dear ones, how many of you are caught up in this senseless game of superiority: 'I am better than you, I am right, you are wrong' or 'I am more spiritual than you.' How can anyone who has studied the sacred teachings truly believe in superiority without doubting the whole concept? This attitude expresses the opposite of humility, Oneness and equality of man, which every religion proclaims as its major foundation. Sadly, almost everyone is carrying these seeds of separation.

It is not only the Orthodox Jews who believe they are the chosen ones or the fundamentalist Muslims calling for Jihad against the disbelievers. No dear friends, it sits in all of you and acts like a toxin. We invite you to identify this poison and eliminate it from your thinking. Whenever you find yourself having thoughts of superiority, remind yourself of the Oneness we all share. Then give this Oneness your undivided attention and truly feel and embrace it, instead of focusing on that which apparently separates you from one another. If you would practise this attitude collectively, wars and destructive disagreements would become impossible once and for all. This alone would bring an end to hatred, blame, attack and fight, and you would cease to steal, betray and lie to your fellow man. You see, all of your intricate religious laws only became necessary because you did not follow the law, that you are all One. Humanity is *one being*! If you would truly understand this, all other laws would not be required.

Many are waiting for our coming. Yet our coming is very different from what you expect. We come as peace, truth and love. Everything that is not in alignment with peace, truth and love cannot maintain its existence in the light of the Divine descending on earth.

Yet we are not interested in destroying your physical temple walls. Our attention is solely focused on assisting you in letting go of unnecessary limiting beliefs, separating you from one another and dividing male from female, black from white, rich from poor, country from country, religion from religion and so on. We are coming to swing the sword of truth. Everything that is not in alignment with truth will fall. You may now say, 'These are only words written on paper — a book someone wrote, claiming that it comes from the Heart of God, which has sent Jesus, Mohammed, Moses, Krishna, Buddha and others. How can we believe this to be true?' Not only are we writing this book, we are all here. Yet this time we are not returning in the shape of the lamb. We come in the splendour of our divine form. Our coming, prophesied long ago is happening *now*! You may expect our arrival to be different, and the use of our divine power might make you feel uncomfortable, but what do you think we are using at this moment as we speak to you? Dear friends, it is the healing power of love that we bring to encourage you to recognise the truth and act accordingly. We need to shake you, to wake you up from your dream of limitation.

In the Bible it is prophesied that there will come a time when there will be many who say they are Christ, but they are false Christs and there will be great confusion. Look around you — are there not many who say they speak in Christ's name and do not act upon his message? Please understand that the Spirit that unites is Christ's spirit, the spirit of love, peace and truth. This will never be any different and it never was. Take this as a measure when you wish to learn about discernment. If something rings true to you, follow it with your heart and soul and become a living example of truth, peace and love.

11

POWER

Many human beings appear to be infatuated with the search for power. This search is fuelled by the underlying feeling of powerlessness and, again, we need to state that you are looking in the wrong place. True power cannot be found outside of yourself and can never be gained through achievements in the world of manifestation. Power can only be uncovered deep within your innermost core. Again, we place the symbol of the Spiral onto the earth — the energy of Source is leaving its imprint of truth on every subject we discuss, so that you remember that everything develops from the inside out.

Draw a spiral and follow its movement. Slowly it increases its radius and widens its influence until it is a centred wave of energy, radiating effortlessly from the core of its very essence. True power comes from within, as does everything else. Humanity: wake up and realise that your focus has to turn within.

Introspection will become a natural and common attitude of all inhabitants of tomorrow's world. You will practise self-reflection everywhere — in business, government, hospitals and schools, and at home. Silence and stillness, which are rarely found on your planet at present, will become a natural and highly valued state of being. Meditation, self-reflection and inner healing will be common practice and taught from a very young age. These practices will build the foundation for inner growth and present you with the keys for your spiritual journey.

In this life and perhaps previous lives you might have experienced varying degrees of power and powerlessness, and have now gained a certain level of understanding regarding this issue. Nevertheless, these experiences have not truly stilled your hunger for power or provided you with a satisfying answer. True power can only be found in the mastery of your three lower bodies and the alignment with your Higher Self. Perhaps you have now walked far enough through the labyrinth of life and been sufficiently lost in its illusions, to be ready for the true search, which begins within.

First you need to get to know yourself. Most of you would like to think that you know yourselves well. We do not agree with you. What the majority of you describe as knowing oneself is not even a scratch on the surface of the vast being you truly are. Your entire identification lies within the mask you have created, to avoid pain rising to the surface and prevent it from becoming visible to the world. Humans have preferred, until now, to hide, even from themselves. You are conditioned to skilfully create a mask promising protection and safety. Generally, you identify with this facade until you have to face the challenges of adversity through serious illness, separation, death or financial problems, forcing you to redefine your values and become more honest and real.

We would love to see you consciously choosing honest nakedness, for this is also more pleasant for others and you. Reflect on how much energy you invest into the creation of the perfect mask. Some of you put up with a dysfunctional marriage or a job you dislike, for it provides you with the desired prestige and allows entry to a certain level of society. Others torture their bodies by starving them into tiny frames — which suit a teenager but are not appropriate for a healthy adult. All of this just to win the competitive game of beauty and success against your peers. Reflect on how much of your attention goes into the creation of your mask compared to the amount of focus you give to healing your wounded heart, nurturing the physical body and mastering your chattering mind to allow Spirit to guide you through the challenges of life. We know the percentage figures and we want you to realise that you waste your precious life by pursuing illusions that cannot hold their promise. No matter how sophisticated this mask may appear, and how much effort, money and time you have invested, this façade cannot protect you from suffering in the long term. It will not keep you safe, neither will it bring inner peace nor provide you with true power or love. And was it not the lack of love and the search for power that was your initial motivation for creating this mask? Even though most of your fellow humans are lost in this preoccupation, we call on you to stop wasting your life energy with these pointless endeavours. Instead, focus on what has true value. Begin with your inner journey and, in time, this will bring you safety from within your heart.

Love, inner peace and true power derive from self-mastery. We are not speaking against the pleasures of the material world; however, we do not support the use of these enjoyments as justification for creating a mask, behind which you hide your pain and lose yourself entirely. What we presently observe is pretence of strength, artificial power and an unknown inner world dominated by fear and chaos, yet what humanity needs is to build its strength from within.

We look at you in a similar manner to the way you would when your own children play dress-ups, pretending to be dangerous pirates, fiercely powerful and even a little cruel. All you perceive in this moment is your vulnerable, cute children of the age of four or five. You, however, have passed the age of dress-ups, so to speak, but still occupy yourself with this pursuit. It is now time to leave this part of your evolution behind. Just as a human child passes through certain stages of growth and inner development, the same applies for humanity as a whole, which is now passing the threshold into a higher vibration. We have mentioned that your childhood has ceased and can only vehemently emphasise this fact. We need you to have greater awareness and maturity about the true nature of life and what this implies for you. You have to consciously walk away from the dream of illusion and wake up!

True power can only be found within and through self-mastery. You might believe that you know what power is, but it is our view that even the most powerful men in your world are only small children in terms of consciousness and far from true mastership. You believe power implies having power over a nation, over an army, over a company or at least over your peers, wife and children. What a fundamental error in thinking. In truth you can never have power over anyone. This whole concept is fear based and illusionary. You can force someone to do what you want them to do, and this can be done with one person or a nation, for most people are disconnected from their divine self — their true power centre. Some might be willing to follow you like sheep, yet this is not true power. It is like little children pretending to have power, but in truth it is nothing more than fear-based control. The power we refer to is the power that derives from self-mastery. The definition of a Master is: one who has mastered himself. When you have completely mastered yourself and are in absolute alignment with Source — there is nothing between you and your true nature — ego filters no longer limit God's light and you recognise your own divinity. No inner obstacles remain to interfere with the transmission of divine light into your physical reality. Then, you and the Divine are one and the light that created all worlds and universes is free to be used by the true Master.

This is how we, the Masters of the past, created miracles. This is how Moses parted the Red Sea and Christ healed the sick, raised the dead and multiplied food and wine. People of the earth, we want you to understand that true power is at hand for all of you, if you master yourself. For one who has mastered himself, all forces of creation lie there in front of him to serve. Everything will — and has to — obey his thoughts. This kind of power might appear miraculous to you. Nevertheless, divine power is only given to one who has conquered his lower nature, and completely healed himself from limitation and the belief in separation.

This is the power of God. It can only be given to one who does not long for power, to one who is love, who radiates peace and emanates truth every second of his existence. This is what all Masters do. Take this as an invitation to reflect on how much time you spend on the invention of an illusion — your mask — and the applause of society, compared to the time you spend on your inner journey. In the future, humanity will use the majority of its time on the latter. Become one of the pioneers of the New World and begin your journey to self-mastery.

12

Connecting With Your Higher Self

We would like to have a closer look at your connection with Source, which also means the connection you have with your true nature. At times this connection is seemingly effortless and on other occasions, despite all well-meaning effort, you feel cut off from your I AM Presence. Yet fierce effort is one of the main reasons hindering the connection, for this behaviour is often driven by underlying feelings of unworthiness, by a variety of negative emotions or even by the intention 'to do the right thing'.

You need to realise that all forms of fear-based effort only disconnect you from who you truly are. We want you to understand that you are loved unconditionally as you are, with all your apparent and hidden imperfections. Relax — and breathe deeply. This is in fact the first step — to relax, trust and know you are loved beyond your imagination. Only when you are in this state of being is true openness created. You are then like a beautiful flower turning your face towards the sun. The sun stands as an analogy for the life-giving force of your Higher Self — you are opening up to your own inner sun.

Effort, as well as all fear-based actions, thoughts and emotions, create an energy shielding you from who you truly are. You can compare this kind of behaviour with the image of a closed fist. How can a closed fist ever receive? You need to become like a flower and open your hands — your energy field — to be able to receive. Everything that is causing tension, effort and unrest derives from fear, and is therefore disconnecting you from your true nature. Even spiritual practices such as meditation or yoga can be fuelled by detrimental effort and therefore will not lead to the desired peace and inner alignment. It is your inner attitude in every moment of your life that determines your connection or disconnection to your Higher Self.

We want you to discover the beauty of a life that comes from alignment with your divine nature. We are not saying that this will not require your concentrated focus and determination or that no effort is necessary. But it is helpful to become aware of the difference between rigid effort — which is driven by fear — and inner focus, born from trust in yourself and the universe. The latter attitude derives from your inner knowing that everything in this vast creation is supporting you.

Bring to mind the two contrasting images of the fist and your open hands. How can you expect to receive if your energy field is shut down through fear and tension or, to express it in different terms, when your hands are closed? So let us examine which attitude disconnects you from the Divine and which one opens you to everlasting peace. Fear, the mother of all negative emotions, has given birth to many children. All negative emotions, thoughts and actions separate you from Source. Every time you judge yourself or others, every time you are angry or hate yourself or others, every time you feel envy or jealousy, you disconnect from the Divine. This is also true for all thoughts of superiority — where you cut yourself off from your own inner light. The list is endless.

Source is pure love, truth and peace. In order to be in alignment with Source, you have to radiate the same frequency as Source — the frequency of peace, truth and love — otherwise your vibration will not be compatible and cannot align with the Divine. This implies that you have to exchange all fear-based emotions, thoughts and actions for those that are more loving and understanding, until you reach pure, unconditional love and lasting inner peace. Then you will know you have returned home and become one with divine bliss. The bliss you experience in orgasm can only give you a faint glimpse of the ecstasy awaiting you, when you truly know who you are.

Positive attitudes such as love, compassion, understanding, support, patience, peace, truth and trust open you like a flower embracing the sun and thus connect you to your True Self. These feelings inspire, guide and provide you with a deep inner knowing that you are unconditionally loved, which in turn connects you even more.

We have now explored various inner attitudes and observed that the frequency level of your emotions and thoughts will determine your connection or disconnection with Source. Let us now examine another component, which is related to time — or to be more precise, speed. What we mean by speed in this regard is the speed at which you walk your timeline and cross the intersections, where we are able to connect, where your timeline and our energy can meet. In the western world you are encouraged to fit as much as possible into your day. In order to fulfil your obligations, you have to be in a rush for most of your waking hours. The demands of your private and professional lives, enforced by your own expectations, have put the majority of you under immense pressure. You seem to live in a hamster wheel, where there is no escape. This illusion is running the life of almost all human beings. We need to tell you that, if you want to connect with your true potential, there is no alternative but to get off this hamster wheel and become still — very still. You are running so fast that you miss everything the universe has perfectly set in place for you to make your life whole and filled with joy and love. In actual fact, you are running too fast! Life has become an effort causing immense inner tension, which closes you off to such an extent that receiving has become an impossible dream. Look around you, there is no time left for anything else. Why do you believe cancer, depression and heart disease are on an explosive rise in all developed countries? It is an outcry from your souls related to your unbalanced lifestyle. It is time to rethink your approach to life.

In truth, the perfect life is already laid out for each one of you as a blueprint on the higher plane. Through connecting to your divine nature you draw this life into your physical existence. Unfortunately, most of you are preoccupied with negative thoughts and emotions and are therefore out of alignment with your Higher Self, and with that you disconnect from this perfect divine plan. As a result, your life drowns in effort, stress and unhappiness, which only create more negative emotions and further disconnection. Sadly, this is the situation the majority of humanity faces today. In order to link with Source — your divine self — you need to stop racing through your life as if there is no tomorrow and become still. Slow down, relax, breathe and smile — a silent smile. This is the beginning. These are the first steps in remembering who you are. There is not only life after death; there is also a beautiful life laid out in divine perfection by your own I AM Presence as a blueprint for this life. Yet this life can only manifest when you open up to the Divine.

When speed is disconnecting you from your true nature, what can connect you? It is slowing down and being in the Now! The only moment that truly exists in all of creation is — Now. Because you are rushing with insane pace through life, you are missing this sacred portal — The Eternal Now. This is the only doorway within the illusion of time to connect to All That Is. We are waiting on the other side of the veil — in the timeless eternal reality at the sacred threshold of Now, to assist you in manifesting your divine blueprint. Unfortunately, we only meet every now and then for brief moments when you let go of negativity and slow down — then glimpses of paradise can be given.

Imagine if you would love yourself and creation, be at peace and send out peace to the world, be true to yourself and others, live in the Now — you would experience life in paradise, abundance, joy and effortless ease. You would receive the complete delivery of your divine blueprint. Through your alignment with Source, you would have drawn into manifestation this perfect plan, created by your Higher Self. This is how life is meant to be for each one of you. This is heaven on earth and this is what your Creator wants for you and what you truly desire for yourself. Regrettably, the majority of you only slow down when forced through sickness or other extraordinary circumstances. You also believe that negative thoughts and emotions are an entirely 'normal' occurrence in human life. Therefore, this beautiful life that is meant for each one of you cannot manifest in your physical reality. You close yourself off from heaven with your own unhelpful and destructive behaviour. We, the Enlightened Ones, the inhabitants of heaven, are always — literally every second—there to support your journey to mastery — to assist you to master your physical, emotional and mental bodies and align with your spiritual self. This is the only way to bring heaven to earth and peace to your heart and soul.

13

SELF LOVE

In the previous chapter we spoke about your connection to your Higher Self and the difficulties in establishing and maintaining this vital link. We would like to mention another reason for your disconnection from Source, which is how you relate to yourself. The vast majority of humans do not love themselves, and with that they deny the love they are — the very essence of the Divine.

God loves you unconditionally, just as you are. While the Divine may not always consider your actions to be wise, we do not love you any less. Contrary to this, if you were to discover that you have acted in an inappropriate manner or made a mistake, you would generally judge and withdraw love from yourself. If you do not meet your expectations or miss a set goal, you act in the same manner, and when you can no longer maintain the façade of perfection and lose your rank in the artificial hierarchy of society, you label yourself as a failure. You let yourself down, harshly judge and punish yourself and usually withdraw all emotional support and encouragement.

Regrettably, not only people with worldly ambitions display this self-destructive behaviour; it is also found in the vast majority of spiritual seekers. We would like to give you a few examples that further explain what we mean. For instance, if you experience peaceful meditations or practise yoga or chi gong, you feel content with yourself, yet as soon as negative emotions such as anger arise — interrupting your serene state of being — you begin to judge yourself.

Generally, when negative emotions surface, most of you either deny these unwanted feelings or even condemn yourselves as not being spiritual enough. You act the same way when you believe you have failed to achieve your expectations concerning spiritual goals, not realising that you might have used these goals to cover up issues of unworthiness. You abandon yourself when things do not work out as planned or you are unable to act in accordance with your inner dictator, who often wears the mask of a monk or nun. Then you withdraw love and understanding from yourself instead of supporting and encouraging this part, which desperately needs your love. In fact, this aspect is the missing link to your greater wholeness.

We wish to encourage you to begin there — exactly there — in this very moment when disappointment over your shortcomings and so-called failures seems to overwhelm you and lead to loveless judgment. Pause and become aware that this behaviour towards your imperfections is not only disconnecting you from the Divine but also from yourself as a human being. Open your heart to this abandoned part. Love, understand and literally embrace and hold it — call the Divine to shower this wounded aspect with white golden healing light. This is not difficult to do; in fact it is simple, and yet these steps will reverse the lock you have placed on our connection. Then divine energy can again flow between us, for you have opened up to love — our most powerful link.

All human beings are longing for love, but most of you believe it is the longing for someone to love you. In truth it is your deep unconscious longing for you to love yourself with all of your imperfections. Only loving yourself unconditionally will make you whole. In general, you project this longing onto your external world and thus created the story of the 'white knight' or 'the most beautiful woman' who will 'save' you. On a deeper level, the majority of you can identify with the principle of this story, even though few would freely admit it. How many of you secretly believe that, if only the right woman or man would come into your life, everything would be fine? Yet 'the right woman/man' is your own inner female/male energy that needs to reintegrate within you. It is about you, loving yourself home. No-one else can do this for you, not even the most charming knight or the most beautiful woman.

You are called to wake up from the hypnotising dream, keeping your attention fully focused on the external world. The world of outer manifestation is only a reflection of your inner world. If you do not change your perspective, you will remain stuck entertaining yourself with fighting your own shadow and continue to project the longing for your True Self onto other people in your life. This game can only lead to disappointment and will be followed by complaints that the victims of your projections are not fulfilling your dreams. Wake up and realise that you are not treating yourself the way you would wish others to treat you. What you truly need is first to love yourself unconditionally. Your surroundings can only reflect what you do unto yourself. This is universal law.

It is truly time for humanity to rise above their ignorance and study the laws of the universe. While you know how to build rockets and fly to other planets, you do not know yourself nor do you understand the spiritual principles upon which this world and all other worlds are built. We invite you to overcome this ignorance and lead a peaceful and fulfilling life by practising the insights you have gained.

14

THE LAWS OF LIFE

We have talked on the subject of alignment to Source — how this will bring your divine blueprint into manifestation and the need for your preparation on all levels for this to happen.

Remember, only the Divine, the One That Was Never Born and Can Never Die, is worthy of devotion. Therefore do not worship the Masters who have found their way home. It would be like a small child imagining his father as almighty, for he does not know better. This is exactly what has happened to Christ, Buddha and other enlightened teachers. We do not judge you for this behaviour, as we are aware that your actions are determined by your level of consciousness. The vast majority of human beings are almost entirely lost in the collective unconscious and out of alignment with their divine nature. Enlightened beings like us, when incarnated as Jesus, Mohammed, Buddha and others, lead extraordinary lives, yet it was never our intention to be worshipped. By no means did we want you to follow, like blind sheep, an ever-growing spiritual doctrine developed from our original teachings. These core teachings explained the basic laws of the universe and creation, its application as well as various pathways to true inner freedom. First, you were taught how to relate these laws to yourself and then how to interact with the world accordingly. This is our true legacy. For instance, we did not teach you not to love the woman your heart has chosen, but we did advise you not to lose yourself in this strong emotion perceived as love. Neither did we recommend wearing a yellow, white, black, brown or red robe — which was the case with most religions, preferring one colour over the other and then having an explicit spiritual explanation for their choice, which later developed into a rule of their order.

Wake up, humanity, and realise that the teachings you have received, handed down for thousands of years, have been altered, censored and manipulated and now have little resemblance to our original message, which has existed throughout eternity as the core of truth. Yet the essence of our sacred teachings can still be found within all of your holy books. You have become lost in translation, in outer rituals and within your stone temple walls. This is not what Buddha wanted, nor Jesus, Mohammed, Krishna or Moses or any of the Enlightened Ones — we came to earth to teach you the path to freedom, inner peace, stillness of mind and a loving heart. These are the basic requirements for your realignment with Source.

We are now collectively raising our voices and ask you to rethink what is the truth in your religious teachings. Answer the following questions: 'What is the reason for this practice? Where do these teachings lead me?' If these spiritual beliefs teach you to be more loving, peaceful, compassionate and truthful, we encourage you to continue. If, however, these teachings lead you to self-righteousness, arrogance and artificial superiority, discard them from your life. These teachings and practices have no value in the eyes of the Almighty One.

It does not please our hearts when we see brother fighting against brother in physical, emotional or mental battles. Sadly, this is largely our observation. You seem to fear each other greatly. You are at war with yourselves, just as you are with your fellow humans. How can any religion postulating love, peace and truth actually preach or bless war against another religious group? Nevertheless, almost all religions created in our names have practised exactly this attitude against one another throughout the centuries. We wish to see an end to this immoral tradition.

Already our light shines bright upon the earth. Soon the light of truth, peace and love will make wars impossible once and for all. Every arrow of aggression sent out to harm another human being, whether on a physical, emotional, mental or spiritual level, will instantly return to you like a boomerang. There will no longer be 'the mercy of time delay'. When we remove this instrument of grace, every action will virtually have immediate consequences for all of you. In fact, actions have always had consequences, but there was divine mercy and grace set in place to allow you to experience the results of your deeds as time delayed. We are gradually removing this 'instrument of mercy', for you did not learn. Divine grace protected you from the immediate consequences of your behaviour, just as a mother would put a pillow on the floor to cushion the fall of her baby.

Yet, as we have mentioned earlier, your childhood has ceased. There will no longer be cushions to soften your fall. When you fall, you will fall and experience the floor as hard. In this way you will have the opportunity to learn how to prevent pain in the future. You need to recognise the direct connection between your actions and the resulting events occurring later in your life — apparently coincidentally. There are no coincidences! This term you have invented refers to a mental construct that does not exist. Every one of you attracts that which you love and fear the most as well as the consequences of previous actions. This is called 'the Law of Karma'. So, there are no coincidences, there is only the screen you call life, where the universal laws are playing out. Whether you believe or doubt what we have just said, nothing will alter the fact that every situation in your life is created by these laws. So, why would you not wish to become more familiar with 'the Divine Principles of Creation' to enable you to better deal with the challenges of life?

You study to become a doctor, a mechanic, a dentist, a teacher and so on and send your children to school to learn about maths, reading, writing, literature, sport, physics, biology, history, art and many other subjects, but few see the importance of understanding 'the Manual of Life', revealing the secrets of how to truly live. All of your holy books contain the wisdom and knowledge for your return to Source. Yet, in taking the teachings too literally, the outer traditions were lost in translation, while on the other hand the true teachings were kept alive by mystics and secret orders, preserving the truth since the beginning of time.

Should 'the Science of True Life' not be the first thing you learn when you begin your education? Would this knowledge not help you to better understand yourself, your fellow humans and life? We are not proposing that you do not aim for a good education and career. Yet, in studying the true 'Laws of Life', your chosen pursuit as a human being would be more rewarding, for you would become a wiser doctor, a more loving teacher, a compassionate business leader and a truly content human being.

We are aware that we might appear hard to please and could be perceived as overly critical. This is not our intention. We do not judge you. We only wish to share our observations regarding the true origin of your problems, for we see that even human beings with the best intentions are looking for solutions in the wrong places.

As the great scientist Albert Einstein once said, 'We cannot solve our problems in the same state of consciousness in which we created them.' His statement captures the essence of our message, the purpose of our conversation. Our wish is to support you in raising your consciousness, for you cannot find the solutions your world desperately needs to solve its current difficulties when the majority of its inhabitants are completely out of balance. In fact you need to make this leap in consciousness if you want to survive as a human species. It would be wise to leave your spiritual ignorance behind and study 'the Eternal Laws of Life' that rule throughout creation.

This transmission is more than an invitation — it is a celestial call! We are calling all souls to wake up from their slumber — walk the way you talk — and ask: 'Why was I born?' — 'Who am I?' — 'What is the purpose of my life?'

15

THERE IS ONLY LOVE

There is only love. Love is All That Is. For some of you this declaration might sound idealistic when you consider the atrocities and suffering on earth. Yet it is not our intention to ridicule you, so lend us your ears — open your hearts and listen to what we have to share. These insights might help you to see difficult future events in a different light — situations you might have labelled a disaster may then be seen as less painful — perhaps even as rewarding and opportunities for inner growth.

Suffering arises through resistance to what is. We would like to teach you to lessen your resistance towards unwanted life situations and encourage you to see with our eyes, which only perceive love regardless of all external circumstances. You might wonder how this can be possible when one is aware of the appalling extent of pain and suffering on this planet. Know that we feel total compassion for every human soul and we do not question the authenticity of your pain. Yet most of your suffering arises through resistance to what is and another factor — ignorance. This ignorance does not acknowledge the wise guidance of your soul and the loving hands of the Divine, which provide you with the exact circumstances as learning opportunities for unconditional love. Understand — the Divine only has your inner growth in mind and will do whatever is necessary to lead you there.

As a consequence of your ignorance of what life wants to teach, many of you get trapped in pain and are unable to look behind the scene where 'a loving parent' is inventing a kind of puppet theatre so that you may learn an important lesson. Yet in this case the parent is your own soul and Higher Self. Does this mean that you have put these painful events in place? Indeed, this is exactly how it is. Your soul, under the guidance of your Higher Self, provides all of these situations to assist your utmost inner growth. Your soul and Higher Self do this out of love for you so that you, as their 'soul extension' in incarnation, can heal and realign with your divine self and return to where you once originated — the unlimited, almighty ocean of divine consciousness.

In seeing life through our eyes, you may for instance discover that the death of a loved one might come into your life allowing you to learn about the great mystery of death. You might still feel or even have psychic contact with this person you love, after he has left the physical body. As a result you review your beliefs about death and discover that death does not exist in the sense that you previously believed. Or you may have to separate from someone against your will and through this painful process you gain a more profound understanding of who you are. You may realise how you have mistaken true love to mean giving your power away. As a consequence of this insight, you embark on a healing journey to find yourself more deeply than ever before. What appeared to be a catastrophe in the beginning has in hindsight revealed itself as a true blessing. Have some of you not experienced simular situations?

In actual fact, every situation and everyone coming into your life is a blessing, and solely there for you to grow — learn to love, forgive and be true to yourself. Everything in your life is arranged in divine perfection to make you whole and bring you closer to your true nature. So whenever you feel resistance towards someone, or a frightening and painful situation is occurring, take a deep breath and pause. Remove your attention from the outside world and turn inwards. Find the sacred portal of your heart to the realms of wisdom and peace. Enter the space of stillness beyond silence. Only there will you be able to comprehend the true intentions of your soul and Higher Self, who agreed, prior to your incarnation, that these events would take place. To connect with us you have to step back from the noise of the external world and enter the sacred chamber of your heart. We will lend you our eyes and you will realise that even behind the deepest pain there is only God's love and wisdom guiding you into greater awareness — into greater life.

Call upon us when resistance and pain drown you in an ocean of fear and you become blind to what is real. We will be there to gently open your eyes to the deeper meaning that is disguised by external events, and reveal your learning opportunity. Then you might realise how much your trust has grown — after losing your financial security for example. Trust, previously anchored in material wealth, is now anchored in inner safety, born from the belief in yourself and the Divine. You will recognise that your heart has truly opened since it was broken because you lost someone you love. You will become aware of all the blessings birthed from these unwanted situations and begin to see the real world that lies beyond the noise of your own world. Your external life is nothing but a perfect stage, an illusion, a living hologram created by you — for you — to expand your consciousness. When you enter the real world, you will realise that there is nothing but Love. There Is Only Love. Love is All That Is!

We invite you to ask for guidance in every situation where resistance and confusion overwhelm you and cause suffering. Connect with us through your heart and you will receive an answer. You will observe painful and difficult situations turning into tools for healing. Deepest wounds will transform into the source of your greatest strengths. You will walk through life with less and less resistance until there is only an unconditional 'Yes' to life. When there is nothing and no-one left, you cannot love; you will perceive everyone and everything through the eyes of love and know that you are home.

We already feel waves of joy from the celebrations singing throughout all universes for your homecoming! We know you will come to this point in consciousness — sooner or later. Time does not exist where we come from, just here on this stage named earth. We wait for you in heaven.

16

YOU ARE UNDER RECONSTRUCTION

We would like to offer you further explanation as to what has been unfolding concerning the prophesied shift on earth. The current situation could be compared to a global building site. Imagine your planet as a beautiful but old palace — a little run down and without modern facilities such as bathrooms, plumbing and electricity. You wish to restore this wonderful palace, for you love its atmosphere and beauty, but the whole building needs an upgrade to modern-day standards. Have you ever been on the site of an old home that is being restored? We assume most of you have, and ask that you remember your first impressions. At certain times did it not look more like 'a destruction site' than a building site? Well, this is exactly what we are pointing out, so that you fully understand the gravity of this global and personal transformation that is currently under way.

Dear ones, you are all under reconstruction — the whole planet is under reconstruction. This is the reason why many things do not seem to make sense. Little seems to function as it did before — not even the weather patterns. It appears that all is being shaken and the very foundation of life is becoming increasingly unstable. This is indeed the case, and it is happening with the full consent of your souls. You might wonder why your souls would have agreed to experience such unsettling times. What could be the possible benefit?

To find a satisfying answer, let us return to the analogy of the building site. Before the restoration can begin, you first have to remove all that is unstable and dysfunctional. In some cases the electrical system needs replacing and the house has to be rewired. You may have to pull the roof off and build a new one, and reinstate rafters, old windows and even doors. In order to begin the restoration you first need to dismantle and clear the debris from the building site. This process can be used as a metaphor for what is happening on your physical, emotional, mental and spiritual levels, assisting your awakening and realignment with Source.

Unprecedented events are shaking the very core of your identification with yourself or what you perceive as 'you', with the sole purpose of freeing you from flawed concepts and encouraging the replacement of your mask with your True Self. For instance, people who challenge you might come into your life and 'press your buttons' to allow you to get in touch with your deepest fears and hidden pain. This is for one reason only: that you become aware of the unhealed wounds preventing your greater wholeness. Your life is a living hologram, where the illusion named 'Lila' or 'Maya' in the Hindu tradition is set in place in divine perfection. This celestial game has but one goal: for you to grow more whole and release limiting behaviour patterns, attachments and fears. The light flooding your planet is enforcing this process.

What is happening to you individually and collectively is strongly related to frequency. The frequency on this planet has gradually increased over the last few decades. You have now reached the point where nothing can or will remain the same. The time has ceased where you could afford spiritual slumber and cosily rest in your comfort zones. Soon every single soul will feel the impact of this influx of light.

You are experiencing the deconstruction of all that is no longer serving you on a physical, emotional, mental and spiritual level. This dismantling process can be done either with your agreement and insight into its healing nature and necessity, or it will unfold without your conscious consent, causing confusion and other unsettling emotions to surface. You have the choice to embrace the process or remain oblivious to this powerful shift that is unfolding, regardless of your decision. On a higher level, your souls have all agreed to partake in this extraordinary spiritual transformation. Remember, nothing can happen against the free will of your soul — this is divine law.

Let us now return to the image of the building site. Some of you are at the stage of removing all that is no longer functioning. At first glance the whole place looks chaotic, as if you are destroying the house — and in actual fact you are destroying what no longer serves you. In the Hindu tradition this aspect is called Shiva or Kali. In the ancient times this aspect of destruction was understood as necessary and useful — if done for the purpose of renewal and revival. When translated to what is happening on earth, it means that the uncertainty accompanying the deconstruction of the old is necessary and unavoidable, but of a temporary nature. This process will last only as long as it takes to release your attachments and false identification. It also prepares you for a new way of relating to the world, your fellow humans and yourself. It is the first step needed in rebuilding your inner house, based on the principles of truth and love, in order to provide you with true stability. You will no longer have to rely on the empty promises of your mask and the resulting disappointment.

Yet many of you behave like house-owners who are unaware of their building's reconstruction. You complain about the mess and noise, want to keep everything as it was and even shed tears about the apparent 'destruction' of your home. You cannot comprehend the vital purpose of this process and thus remain unable to recognise that it in fact serves the improvement of your house. So you continue with pointless complaints and remain in a state of confusion and inner resistance, leading only to further misinterpretations and discontent. This analogy reflects how the majority of the inhabitants on earth react to the events set in place to serve your inner and outer 'reconstruction'.

We wish to remind you that everyone chose to be here at this time and gave permission to partake in this transformation. You were all keen to incarnate and participate in these extraordinary times. We invite you to call upon us whenever negative emotions overtake you; we will then enable you to see with clarity and you will gain insights of higher wisdom.

Understand that humanity and planet earth are under reconstruction in order to raise their frequency. This process is fully under way. There is no returning to the old ways. Metaphorically speaking, we have already torn the walls down, pulled out the broken pipes and dismantled the roof. We know you feel uncomfortable — out of your comfort zone — and this is good, for in your comfort zone you do not grow, you do not learn. In some of you 'the rewiring process' has already begun and 'new walls' have been built. In the case of a few, 'a new roof' has been installed and the renovation is nearing completion. All unfolds according to your willingness or resistance, which is determined by your level of consciousness.

All events in your life serve to awaken you to your true potential. As we mentioned at the beginning of our conversation, we do not promise you a walk in a rose garden. At least not yet, for you are in the middle of the greatest collective transformation this planet has ever seen. After the hard work is done, your inner and outer worlds *will* be like a rose garden, where peace, love and truth reside. You will birth heaven to earth through your own beingness. Until then, there is work to be done. This work can only succeed if you are well informed and consciously heal yourself and thus lessen your resistance towards this sacred transformation.

Remember, everything in your life is set in place by the Divine with only one goal — to provoke you into deeper love, peace and truth and to bring you home. The highway to heaven is only entered through non-resistance. In not resisting what is, you will open your heart and your inner ear and hear the song of your soul, guiding you wisely through the storms of life. Along with your own soul, we sing this song for you.

17

INTEGRITY

We know it is not easy for you to comprehend that the Divine is speaking to you directly. Few can truly believe that this is happening. For us, this is not important. It is only important that you fully understand our teachings and practise them in your daily life. Knowledge stored in your mind, discussed and spoken about has no value in the eyes of the Divine — it does not belong to you. You need to live what you know and believe — this is integrity. Then you will own this knowledge and the teachings will become alive in you. You will be a living example of peace, love and truth. This is the true meaning of the term 'the living Bible'. This is who we are and what we invite you to become.

Live what you believe to be true. Stop feeding your overloaded mind with more knowledge if you are unable to put it into practice. Furthermore, stay away from fruitless and theoretical spiritual discussions. Do not try to convince others with words; instead live according to your beliefs and so become a living example of truth. This will attract the attention of your fellow humans. They will feel the difference in you and might want to know where your peace, strength and love come from. Then you may speak of your inner journey and your words will have power. Can you see the difference between preaching and teaching? A true teacher never preaches, for he knows when a soul is ready. A true teacher walks the way he talks whereas a preacher talks of what he is still dreaming. How can he know the feeling and describe the view from the top of mountain when he has still not climbed to the peak himself? He cannot. The preacher only refers to the knowledge of others who have found the path to freedom. Know that a teacher can only guide you to the point of consciousness he has personally reached. The rest is left to interpretation and speculation.

Unfortunately, this is how all religious systems were established in our names. We climbed to the top of the mountain, described to our students the path and shared the view we enjoyed as we reached the peak. As time passed by, the disciples of the disciples, and then their disciples and so on, interpreted and speculated about the view from the top of the mountain. They could no longer discern truth from tales. How could they? It is impossible to know how you feel at the summit when you have only passed the first third of your climb or barely begun your journey. Even on the final third, the joy, freedom and breathtaking perspective you experience at the peak are unimaginable.

As it is with a mountain expedition, so it is with your spiritual journey: the last third is the steepest and the student needs to concentrate very hard on every step. He has to live minute by minute and rely on total trust to survive. Only living in the eternal Now will open the gateways to the universal knowledge the initiate requires to pass through the final stage of his journey. He has to give everything just to climb a little further. We ask you now, how can a student who is having this extreme experience know what it looks and feels like to be at the top of the mountain? He cannot — his interpretation will always be tainted by his effort, exhaustion and concentration, which are absolutely necessary for the final part of the journey. When your consciousness has reached its zenith and you are 'the Master of the world' — your own world — all effort falls away. You have conquered yourself; you have mastered yourself. You are free from the bondage of illusion. Now you understand; no words need be said. You are All That Is, Ever Was And Ever Will Be.

Only an enlightened teacher can give you the direct teaching. Anyone with a lesser consciousness than an enlightened one has to rely on interpretation and speculation. He may offer interesting philosophies about the path and goal, but his views are not underpinned through the direct experience of absolute freedom. In actual fact, they do not know what they are talking about. No-one knows what he has not experienced personally. Well-meaning students have established organisations from our teachings, which later developed into religions, made us their leaders and provided you with second-hand knowledge. Yet this knowledge is not real. Sometimes, it has even gone as far as turning our teachings into the exact opposite. Someone who has not attained mastership cannot teach you to become a Master. Someone who has not mastered himself is not a Master. It is that simple. Truth always speaks for itself.

Yet our true teachings survived, hidden in the underground, taught by high-level initiates to their students — often in fear for the safety of their lives. These mystery schools were opposed and often persecuted by the religious establishment that directed and controlled the masses. As we have previously mentioned on several occasions, all that is not aligned with truth, peace and love cannot be taken into the new world, for the New Earth is vibrating on a higher frequency. Established religious systems will have to change dramatically or they will vanish from the face of this planet. All religions that do not serve the sacred paradigm will fall, as will everything that does not raise its frequency.

You may ask yourself, who then will teach us? We, the Divine itself and all of our master aspects, which can be directly accessed through prayer and meditation. We are here for every human soul who is ready to study the laws of true life. Your heart is like a sacred mobile phone and our number is already stored. You only have to open your heart and call upon us — we hear you, regardless of where you are. We will always listen and offer our guidance. You may have to train to perceive our voices clearly, for your ears are so used to the noise of the world. It takes patience, perseverance and practice to hear the voice of silence whispering in your heart, but only through the heart is direct communication with the Divine possible.

You might also join one of the study groups for spiritual development that are becoming more popular. However, be mindful not to give your power away, for the time of the guru has ended. Know that spiritual teachers and gurus are only your older brothers and sisters guiding you to your own light. Learn discernment. Be careful if someone tries to direct your focus onto the brightness of his own light. Be aware that this person has something to learn about the illusion of his spiritual ego. Learn to go deep inside, open, expand, heal and purify your heart, and our voice will be heard a little more clearly each time you call us. You will recognise our Presence by the peace in your heart while we are communicating. Close the window to the external world — which does not mean you have to become a recluse — and enter the portal to the sacred world of your heart. Dial our number by opening your heart and you will receive guidance.

We wish to reveal a secret to you. It is the sacred promise, given to humanity from the beginning, that God is there for you. Every true spiritual teaching was speaking of this simple movement towards the inner world. There, in your innermost core, your true divine teacher waits patiently for you to be ready. The Divine was and is always there, but many of you preferred to pursue the entanglements of life or engaged in religious rules and regulations and in doing so forgot this simple promise from God to his creation. God's love is always there for you! If you truly believed and knew this deep within your soul, you would already be living in paradise. You not only find it difficult to believe that you can personally contact the Divine without the help of a priest, guru or other spiritual teacher, the majority of human beings simply do not trust God. You doubt that God cares for you, loves you and will give you all you need in divine perfection. Let us give some thought at another time to this deep pain, which sits in all of you. In the meantime please accept our love.

18

YOU DO NOT TRUST GOD

You do not trust God. You do not trust your Almighty Creator. This is a bold statement. Despite all prayers, meditations and various spiritual practices, most of you still have not healed the deepest wound, the core of your split inside — your distrust in God — the pain of separation from Source. Most of you have a greater trust in your insurance company than you do in God. Here lies the root cause of your pain. Unconsciously, you all believe deeply in the illusion that you are separate from the Divine. You are convinced you are not good enough and you have to work hard to become worthy of God's love. How absurd, when you as human parents love your children regardless of what they do. How could it be possible that we as your 'divine parents' put conditions on our love? Do your children have to be perfect? Do they have to work hard to earn your love? Or do you just love them as they are?

This love was there for them from the moment they were born. This love arose from your heart effortlessly without your willing it into life. Well, this is how it feels for us, too. We love you. Sometimes we may shake our heads when we look at you, as all parents do. On other occasions we are very pleased when you remember more and more of who you are, but neither our approval of you nor our critical observations influence the love constantly pouring from the Heart of God to all of you.

So why do you doubt that you are loved, that God cares and is there for you? The connection between us is always intact from our side. Since your creation, the Divine has always been open and in steady contact with you. But from your side it has been a different scenario. We watch you running, trying to hide, feeling unworthy — not spiritual enough, imperfect, unlovable. These are just a few examples of the countless negative messages arising continuously from humanity's subconscious. Do you know what is happening energetically when you send out these negative thought forms with corresponding emotions? It is like a flower completely closing off from the sun. You shut all of your petals, which are supposed to bathe in the rays of the sunlight. If you believe you are imperfect, unlovable, unworthy of God's love, you cut yourself off from the Divine, and confirm with these negative thoughts your existing flawed beliefs. As a result of these negative vibrations you feel even more separate and alone, and God does not seem to exist. It feels like nobody cares and you have to put in so much effort to get somewhere, anywhere. These destructive internalised beliefs further confirm your fears and will manifest in your life — a self-fulfilling prophecy.

The only way out of this dilemma is to stop giving energy to these limiting thoughts and emotions and replace them with positive truthful affirmations such as:

1. I am unconditionally loved with all that I am by the Divine every second of my life, since ever and forever.
2. There is no separation between the vast consciousness I call God and me — we are one.
3. I am cared for and loved by my Creator.
4. I am Love.

All you have to do is open to the Divine by loving yourself unconditionally. You need to connect to love again, and these affirmations will allow you to do so. Love, support, encouragement, stillness, understanding, kindness, patience, peace with yourself open you up to Source. Self-judgment, feelings of unworthiness, striving for impossible perfection, having high expectations and non-forgiveness cut you off from Source. Alternatively you could say: every negative thought and emotion separates you from the Divine, which is who you truly are, whereas positive thoughts and emotions open you up to the Divine.

The belief of never being good enough seems deeply ingrained in the human psyche. How can these negative convictions be transformed? The only way to change unwanted emotions is to embrace them. If you fight against them, you will only strengthen what you do not want. So, do not fight, instead love the part that believes in unworthiness. This aspect acts in this manner because it was conditioned this way in order to survive, and this learned behaviour once served you well. But today it sabotages your life and needs healing. Understand this aspect, communicate with it, embrace it and send love. Love, love, love! When this part of you has received enough love, the wound will close and heal. Then you will be able to reintegrate this abandoned aspect into your greater being. This is the only way to cure the split, layer by layer until all of your aspects know that you are one with the Divine and you feel that you can trust your Creator under all circumstances. You will then know with certainty that Source always gives you everything you need in divine perfection.

There is a time for every soul to consciously confront itself with the fact that it does not trust God. When you are ready to do this, it will be one of the most rewarding journeys you have ever undertaken. We want you to thoroughly examine all of the mechanisms you have put in place in order to feel safe. You need to truthfully look at all efforts and achievements, including the most subtle control and manipulation techniques you have developed for your safety, which are acting like a security net for a tightrope walker. In order to heal the split, you need to cure the true cause of your pain. Not only do you have to heal your unloved aspects, you also have to let go of your security net. You need to walk the tightrope without a net.

True trust can only be found in the unknown: in apparent danger, not when you know there is a double net in place in case you fall. True security can only be discovered in your unknown deepest inner core. Only there can you learn to trust where there is no trust, beloveds. This is a journey for the courageous heart, the only path that leads you to true trust, which is freedom itself. He who walks the tightrope until the end has healed his split and restored his trust in the Divine. Your balance will be determined by your belief in the unbelievable and the degree to which you trust the possibility of the impossible becoming your reality. It will depend on your ability to let go of the old mind and unite yourself with the Divine. You are the only one vehemently denying this union. Walk, dear ones, into the unknown. Only there will you find the long-lost attributes of a spiritual warrior, a Christ in kindergarten stage. Trust where there is no trust. Then you will discover that you are looked after in the most caring way every second of your life. You have never been alone, for we carried you when you were too weak to walk on your own.

You will also realise that the human mass consciousness is trapped in the greatest illusion by believing in separation from Source. You will laugh with us when you arrive on the other side of the veil and pierce through this illusion. The experience of discovering your Oneness with the Divine — the fact that you are divine — Love itself looking after itself — is possible through the pathway of initiation during this lifetime. You do not have to postpone this realisation until the process of transformation you call death, when these insights are often natural. Then you will truly understand the deeper meaning of Jesus saying that man has to die and be born again to enter his kingdom. Your laughter will be echoing loud throughout the universe. You will know you are free, and will wonder how you could ever have believed in being separate from Source? How you could ever have not trusted in God? How in the world could you ever have believed that you are not good enough to be loved? It will seem that you can no longer remember the answer.

19

YOU ARE LONGING FOR YOUR TRUE SELF

Dear ones, regardless of what you are longing for and trying to achieve in life, it is in its essence your masked yearning to return to Source — your true nature. Every time you fulfil a desire, reach a goal or materialise a dream, you still find yourself dissatisfied and searching for more. In actual fact, no human love or material achievements can still your deepest longing, only the union with the Divine.

You travel along the path of life from one desire to the next, one goal to another, hungry and discontented, rarely at peace with yourself. You will continue to repeat this cycle until you turn inwards and realise that what you were really looking for with all of your goals and achievements was not there to be found. A fulfilled desire always leaves you craving for more, until you understand that what you were longing to find in your partner or your career was in truth your true Self. You then realise that all your striving to achieve in the material world was to gain acknowledgment and love. You tried to be loved through attaining desirable social status, wealth, financial security, titles and more — all of this effort to cover up a part in you that believes it is not loveable. Despite all external success and acknowledgment, you still did not feel loved. All of your accomplishments in life did not help you to find true inner peace nor allow you to experience happiness beyond reason and inner freedom.

Only when humanity becomes aware of the underlying motivation of the unending search that has acted as the main driving force in their lives, will they arrive at a point in consciousness where they no longer become involved in relationships as a poor substitute for their missing connection to their true Self. From this moment onwards your partnerships will improve greatly, for they are no longer burdened by unrealistic expectations, trying to fill the void within. In the near future human beings will investigate with great discernment their outer as well as their inner lives. They will understand that they were searching in the wrong place for fulfilment and realise how they overburdened each other with the projections of their unlived and wounded aspects. Then you will be able to take a relationship for what it is — an equal exchange between two beings on their spiritual journey, where you can support and enrich each other's lives.

Dear ones, your relationships are not working because the relationship between your human part and your Divinity is not working. Your partnerships are only an outer reflection of your inner connection to yourself. Most human beings are currently unaware of the necessity for spiritual alignment and emotional healing, so it happens that one dysfunctional human being connects with another dysfunctional human being and both project their unlived dreams, hopes and fears onto each other. For a short time, during the honeymoon period, this practice seems to work well, because your hearts are open and you tap unknowingly into the full potential of each other's Higher Self. But after a while your hearts close and the love experienced in the beginning fades away and disappointment fills your home.

What you are doing cannot work. For two beings to live together in a long-lasting and truly loving relationship, each individual has to commit to their own spiritual journey and inner healing. On this path you can support each other, but you also have to accept that certain stages have to be walked alone. This does not necessarily mean separation, but requires respect and trust in one another. Unfortunately, most couples develop varying degrees of control systems for each other. Yet control stems from fear and fear opposes love — how can you expect a loving relationship when you do not live the principles of love? If you want to experience love with your partner or anyone else, you need to practice love. Be love — breathe love — live love. You have to become what you are looking for. Nothing can be given if you do not first give it to yourself and share it generously with others.

If you send out a frequency of anger, accusation and expectation as well as a mixture of attack and defence, what do you believe the response will be? Relationship difficulties, fruitless discussions, attack and defence from the other half of the couple are the predictable reactions. Whenever you find yourself in situations like this, take time to reflect and observe. Do not get consumed by strong emotions; instead become conscious of your own negative charge and shift your energy if you wish to improve the situation. Love can only be experienced when you are love. Even if your partner is at first unwilling or unable to cooperate, continue to send out love, understanding and kindness and keep your heart open. Realise how often you close your heart and yet demand love and openness from others. This attitude cannot and will never succeed.

Another widespread misunderstanding concerning relationships is the belief that the partner can overtake responsibility for you. No-one can walk your path for you. Marriage or living in a committed relationship does not mean that you are one being. You are two separate individuals who have met to support one another to grow more whole. The purpose of your meeting is not, as many of you unconsciously believe, that your partner is there to live your unlived sides. The admirable attributes of your beloved are only there to encourage you to develop these within yourself. This is the reason why opposites attract each other: in order to benefit from the differences. In a healthy relationship, two beings inspire one another to expand in consciousness and grow as much as possible into their own wholeness. Unfortunately, most partnerships on earth display varying degrees of co-dependency and emotional imbalances, which only lead to power games.

If you wish to have a loving relationship, we encourage you to overcome the widespread ignorance by studying the true meaning of life and begin your inner healing. Only from a foundation of constant development of self-love, self-appreciation, self-support and self-encouragement can true love with another person be established. Until you understand and practise this lesson, your divorce rates will continue to rise and unnecessary pain and suffering in relationships will maintain their undesirable presence on earth.

Buddha taught that suffering stems from ignorance. All sacred spiritual teachings speak from this eternal truth. Beloveds, it is time to learn about true life. The age when ignorance and fear ruled the earth has ceased. Truth is now descending, love will hold the power on earth and an unwillingness to grow will have consequences. Earth is changing, far beyond what you believe. We are here, serving with truth and love, preparing you for the times to come. Without the appropriate groundwork, life will become very inconvenient and unhealed emotions will cause avoidable suffering and instability. Wake up! Hear our call! A new world is emerging and this new world needs a new human race.

20

BOUNDARIES

We consider the ability to set boundaries as one of the most important basic human skills for leading a healthy life. In fact, you owe it to yourself and others to place appropriate boundaries as a sign of true love and respect. Let us examine this interesting topic, for most of you have difficulty in understanding its necessity and proper use. You need boundaries to protect yourself, to express self-love and self-respect and to signal to others when your space is being invaded. Yet there appears to be a lot of confusion around this issue and few have mastered its lesson.

The difficulties you experience stem largely from the fact that no-one taught you how to put boundaries in place. As a result, most of you remained unaware of their importance and you tried to protect yourself through other means when your space was invaded. We could also say you were left to your own devices and as a consequence boundaries were placed either too late — and with unnecessary force — or not at all.

Let us focus our attention on your childhood, where your story and all learning for this life began. Most human beings experience invasion as small children, for your sense of boundaries does not exist when you are born. Before you take on a human body you come from Oneness and perceive everyone as part of this Oneness. As a baby, you have no sense of boundaries and totally rely on the love and care of your parents. Yet your parents were not taught how to love, protect and respect themselves, so despite all well-meaning effort they invaded their child's space without being aware. For most parents, invasion on an energetic, emotional or even a physical level seems to be entirely legitimate behaviour. We would like to see a change of conduct in this respect, for the early stages of childhood provide the foundations for your whole life.

For now we do not wish to examine all aspects of early childhood conditioning, but will only address the manner in which to place appropriate boundaries. So let us focus on your life as a small child, a time when most parents seem to believe this little creature is entirely theirs and not a separate human being. They seem to forget that they do not own this life, as their parents had forgotten. This small being only needs unconditional love and support until it can live self-sufficiently. Your children do not belong to you. They dream different dreams and aim for their own goals. What they need is your love, care and respect, and that you express your boundaries as well as valuing theirs as they are developing.

Beloveds, a lot of your current emotional conflicts are a consequence of your ignorance around the subject of boundaries, for you were not properly educated in this regard and in actual fact even prevented from putting boundaries in place as a child. As a result, some of you now mistake an invasion of someone else's space for love, which in truth has nothing to do with love. This is only one example of many false assumptions that will cause problems with your partners later in life, for they will not tolerate your false understanding of love and bluntly call it as it is — an invasion. We know this is a difficult theme to comprehend, for many of you are so entangled in this scenario. Some of you play the invader, others get invaded or tolerate invasion, while many other people feel a strong aversion against this kind of behaviour and simply leave the relationship.

In order to live a healthy life you need to express yourself honestly and speak your truth. If someone is crossing your boundaries, you need to develop the capacity to stop this unwanted behaviour.

Let us further examine what happens when someone invades your space and you have not learned how to put proper boundaries in place. At first you will feel anger. Unfortunately, there is in all human societies a lot of judgment and misunderstanding concerning the meaning of anger and how to deal with it. For this reason the majority of you simply swallow anger, for in most situations an expression of this emotion would be considered inappropriate. What happens if you suppress emotions? Emotions do not just disappear, even though you would like to believe this to be the case.

Everything is energy. Energy always remains as energy. It can modify its form and state of aggregation, but will forever remain energy. This is one of the basic laws of physics. Emotions are nothing but energy, and they linger in your body if not expressed. Unexpressed anger turns into aggression. The suppression of anger takes effort and blocks your throat, heart and solar plexus energy centres (chakras). At a certain point you need to release this emotion, which has changed from anger into aggression, and one of your fellow humans will become the unfortunate victim of this release. In most cases this is not the person who caused your anger in the first place.

Do you realise that the primary emotion of anger — which is simply an alarm signal — transforms into aggression, a secondary and more 'poisonous' emotion? Anger could also be considered as the force to push the invader out of your space, by expressing boundaries in a fair and appropriate manner, whereas aggression holds an energetic imprint of a very different nature.

To gain a better understanding, let us use the analogy of grapes, which, after lying in a barrel for some time, turn into vinegar through the fermenting process, after which the end product has little in common with the original sweetness of the grapes. The same principle applies when comparing anger and aggression. Contrary to the primary emotion of anger, aggression has a sharper energy and requires great effort to control, and its built-up pressure unleashes when finally expressed, for you are simply no longer able to suppress it. You may feel relief, but the setting free of aggression always harms the second player in this scenario. Can you see the difference? The fairness and clarity of anger has disappeared.

So what happens if you have learned to control yourself to such a degree that you are unable to express aggression? You will continue to suppress these harmful emotions and keep them trapped in your body, where they will transform from aggression to inner aggression and turn against you. Long-held aggression is already damaging your physical body to a certain extent; however, inner aggression severely weakens and darkens your emotional and mental fields. Modern medicine is gradually acknowledging inner aggression as one of the main causes of depression and other serious health problems.

If you do not learn how to establish appropriate boundaries and refuse to listen to your anger, you will direct this powerful energy against yourself in the form of self-hatred, self-doubt and self-sabotage.

We believe we have now sufficiently emphasised the importance of healthy boundaries to prevent you from unconsciously laying the foundations for future emotional, physical and mental illness. The lack of this important life skill creates substantial but preventable damage on earth. To change the course of your actions and create a healthier environment, we recommend a more thorough education process regarding the importance of boundaries.

There seems to be a great deal of misunderstanding around anger, which is largely considered an unwanted and heavily judged emotion, too inappropriate to express. Certainly there are appropriate and less appropriate ways of expressing anger, but the emotion itself is neither inappropriate nor useless. It acts as an important warning sign from your emotional body, telling you there is something wrong.

We would like you to understand the actual meaning of your emotions and how to deal with them. We see in the future wonderful shifts occurring from the ignorance surrounding emotions to a true loving understanding. You will cease to cling to desirable emotions and also will no longer push negative feelings away. Instead you will heal and integrate your emotions in a healthy manner.

Remember, only when you practise what you have learned can you gain the benefits of any teaching. If you feed your mind with information without the equivalent actions, the seeds of truth will have fallen on barren ground. Walk the way you talk — these are your keys to heaven.

21

WORRY

We would like to share our view about a common and destructive human habit — worry. You worry too much. Most of you plan and think continuously, imagine every possible eventuality of life and in the end get entirely lost with this preoccupation. In order to live a fulfilling life, you need to give up this unhealthy and time-consuming habit, for it leads nowhere, depletes your energy and only leaves you exhausted and filled with distrust and loneliness.

This behaviour developed in human beings because you neglected and denied your connection with the Divine. You have forgotten that your heavenly Father and Mother care for you and deliver everything you need. As previously explained, you have lost trust in the Divine and no longer believe that the Divine is there and truly cares. In truth, the Divine does nothing else but care for you. In forgetting how to properly use your mind and master your emotions, you leave yourself largely occupied with lack and worry. As you now know, the universe always provides you with what you are energetically sending out, for this is understood by the universe as your desire. Unfortunately, as a consequence of you sending out vibrations of worry and lack, you only attract into your life further lack and more to worry about. These are the fundamentals of the 'Law of Attraction'. Through the ignorant use of your emotions and thoughts you have created a world of lack, which is not what the Divine intended for you. Nevertheless, this is what you have attracted, according to your vibration.

We would like to share with you how life on earth would look if you were to only 'worry' about the one thing that truly matters — your alignment with your Higher Self, your main task on earth. If you would all focus on this important quest, life on your planet would soon turn into paradise. Your life until now has been unnecessarily burdened by effort and distrust. As a result, you have a deeply ingrained belief that you need to work hard to achieve happiness and love. The requirements for accomplishing desired goals vary greatly, depending on the conditioning of the different societies' social and religious structures, which in turn form the building blocks of your belief systems. If you are unable to meet these requirements you might feel worthless and fear that you are going nowhere in life.

We would now like to ask, where did all this effort truly lead you? Are you really happy, feel inner peace and love? Is there joy in your life? We do not see that worry and effort could ever guide you to inner freedom. We would like to show you how to achieve true happiness and inner peace, through letting go of your worries. You need to focus on your realignment with your divine self and learn trust if you wish true happiness to become your reality.

As Jesus said, 'But seek ye first the kingdom of God and his righteousness and all these things shall be added unto you. Take therefore no thought for the morrow, for the morrow shall take thought for the things of itself.' (Matthew, chapter 6 verses 33–4) Throughout the last 2000 years these verses have been discussed countless times, but rarely understood. We would like to reveal the hidden message behind these words. Here lies one of the secrets to true life. This is part of the code to bring heaven to earth. So, what can you do to bring heaven to earth and live in paradise? First, you need to focus on everything that is out of alignment with your true nature. Then, replace these behaviours with attitudes resonating with love. Only then, through your allowance, can the Divine provide you with safety, abundance, joy and peace.

It appears that you have all tuned your radios to the wrong channel and are now bitterly disappointed that you are not receiving what you desire. You need to be aware that *you* are the one tuning the radio — no-one else. There is no evil destiny bringing unwanted events into your life. It is *your* worry, *your* distrust, *your* previous actions, *your* unhealed emotions and *your* random thoughts drawing disharmony into *your* life. In order to receive harmony, love and abundance, you need to learn how to tune your radio. This can be achieved by exchanging inner disharmony with healing love and trust. If you are standing at an inner crossroad, your only question should be: 'Am I in alignment with the Divine if I take this direction in life?' If you practise this way of being with patience and perseverance you will at first see subtle, then great, change occurring. Furthermore, you will also witness a remarkable shift in your life and suddenly see things effortlessly falling into place. Now you are in the flow. Synchronicity will unfold its magic wings and you will learn to follow the sacred signs.

Dear ones, life is meant to be joyful. Look at how often you experience life this way and you will recognise whether you are truly aligned with or disconnected from the Divine. We have previously mentioned that there is a divine blueprint. This blueprint will manifest the more you are connected with your own divinity. Unfortunately, most people's blueprint is never downloaded, for they seldom choose to connect with their true nature. This magnificent plan thus remains dormant in the higher worlds, often waiting for lifetimes until the soul is ready for its spiritual journey to begin. Consequently, most human lives continue to be lives of worry, marked by fierce effort, fear and hope, only causing avoidable suffering and limitation. This is the life humanity has known for thousands of years.

We would like to let you know that now is the time when you are all able to change, begin with your healing journey and follow the path of love. No-one is excluded; everyone is called. Will you hear our call — our invitation to paradise? We have opened the portals to heaven; will you follow us? We would like to welcome you all there. A life of joy, abundance, peace and love awaits you. All dreams you have ever dreamed are gathered there, waiting for you to bring them to life. Yet the choice is yours. Are you willing to replace distrust with trust, fear with love, hatred with forgiveness and vague words with the power of truth in action? Remember, whenever you are not true to yourself, you disconnect from Source and close the portals to heaven. Whenever you allow yourself to dwell on negative thoughts and emotions, you separate yourself from your true nature. Whenever you judge yourself or others, your own life becomes darker and you distance yourself from the fulfilment of your dreams.

Dear ones, wake up and walk the path with the Illumined Ones, your brothers and sisters who paved the way for you long ago. Care about one thing only: that you align with Source and discover your own divinity. There is no other way to bring peace, truth and justice, love and freedom, to your world. Embody your virtues! God will take perfect care of your life if you truly commit to your liberation.

You will live like birds, which do not care about tomorrow, because tomorrow is taken care of by the heavenly Father and Mother. Your divine blueprint will manifest the life you deeply desire and deserve. Yet, as long as you prefer worry over trust and believe you have to do it all alone, this miracle cannot happen. As long as you remain 'tuned into the wrong channel', all will stay the same. So, as always, it is up to you. We love you and wait in the spaceless space beyond time for your arrival home.

22

FEAR

Fear is the main disease on your planet and love will be the cure. Sadly, most human actions are driven by fear. How can your world be at peace and in harmony, if you as its creators are in disharmony and fear is the underlying motivation of virtually all of your conduct? Do you realise that your desire for a better world will remain an unreachable dream if you do not change? Your world is a reflection of your thoughts, emotions and actions. Most of you still do not understand that *you* are creating your world. The vast majority of prayers for a peaceful world come from hearts that are everything else but peaceful.

Dear ones, you need to gain a true understanding of the divine laws upon which everything in the universe is built. Otherwise, you will continue to waste your energy with prayers that cannot be fulfilled. How can peace come to a world at war with itself? These two energies oppose each other and hence are incompatible. You have to become what you want to see in your life and in the world. You must transform into a perfect match for your desires or you will energetically reject what you wish for — like two magnets repelling each other. The universe is always ready to give all that you need, but it is you who close off from heaven's blessings by believing in fear. We observe you praying, wishing, even begging and imploring, but at the same time your energy opposes what you desire. We do not suggest to give up praying — yet it is your energetic disharmony preventing the fulfilment of your prayers.

As long as you have a greater belief in fear than you do in God's love, you will live in a very limited world and suffering will remain your faithful companion. As long as you deny your responsibility as creators of your life, you will remain unable to taste true freedom and inner peace. Since you cannot find peace, you distract yourself with pointless activities and various forms of entertainment, which numb your real feelings. This is the reason why most of you are oblivious to what is truly going on inside: you are too busy to listen to the voice of silence, guiding you to the land of peace.

Yet we wish to remind you that it is not the intent of this conversation to judge you. Judgment is a human attitude that we do not share. We are only interested in revealing the true cause of the apparent miseries on earth.

Let us provide a few examples of false convictions hindering your life. As long as you believe you are not good enough, not smart enough, not successful enough, not beautiful, spiritual or rich enough, which are all blunt statements of fear, your external life will always remain a direct reflection of these limiting beliefs. Our observation is that the majority of you repeat negative thoughts on a daily basis like a religious mantra, completely unaware of their far-reaching consequences. As long as you believe in fear-based limitations, your world will mirror these convictions with alarming results. You harvest what you have sown.

If you could see the world through our eyes, you would be surprised by the widespread misuse of your human energy fields and clearly recognise the devastating consequences. You would feel deep compassion for the suffering on earth, even your own ignorance, and we believe your wish would be to help. This is the reason why we have descended many times into the human form: to show you how to gain freedom from ignorance and suffering.

We have intentionally kept the teachings in this book as simple as possible, so that your mind cannot get distracted by new sophisticated spiritual theories. We believe that your mind entertains itself enough and you already have plenty of these theories in which to indulge. This is a call to walk the way you talk, to live according to your beliefs. Lip-service is useless and powerless. We invite you to enter the stillness beyond silence; we are not interested in spiritual discussions. Live in accordance with your heart and so become a living example of truth, peace and love. We do not wish to found a new religion, sect or ashram. Your heart is your temple. This is the place where your divine self speaks to you. The Divine is present in every human heart, ready to lead you through the challenges of life. You need to open the temple doors to enter this sacred space. Make your daily life a constant worship by being truthful, loving all imperfections — whether within yourself or others — and radiating peace. In doing so, you will become truly receptive to the blessings of the Divine.

When you water the plants in your garden, greet them, nurture them and take their needs as a reminder to nurture yourself. Understand that you cannot flower if you do not love and encourage yourself. When you clean your house, give thought to which of your aspects are in need of cleansing. Contemplate which of your old habits no longer serve your highest good and let them go. When you enter a shop and find the assistant behaving in an unfriendly manner, send out a smile and understanding instead of the so easily available judgment and anger. Be reminded by this person of your own discontent and unfriendliness, needing your love to heal.

Realise that every life is filled with miracles. Your spiritual guru is your daily life, teaching you all the necessary lessons to grow more whole. Life is your spiritual teacher, and it provides you with this perfect individually tailored service for free. Life loves you. God loves you. Now you only have to love all of you. Remember God is All That Is. If you are longing to come closer to God, you need to make a simple but profound step — to love all of you, without exception. This is how the Divine loves each and every one of you. Love all imperfections and you will feel peace and intimacy with the Divine.

The obsession of the western world with youth and outer beauty only reflects how little you understand true beauty. True beauty comes from within — from the perfect harmony of form, colour, vibration, inner balance and love. Artificial beauty, as worshipped through the newly founded beauty industry, can be considered as nothing more than a cover-up of the inner disharmony in the individual. This approach will never lead to true beauty, which can only be birthed from within.

We hope that your hearts were open while reading this discourse and we ask that they remain open, for an open loving heart is unable to house fear. As we mentioned in the first line of this chapter, fear is your disease and love will be the cure. Opening your heart is the first step on your journey to love. Love is what you are. By believing in fear, you deny your true nature, your own divinity.

23

JOY

It appears that joy and happiness are considered by the vast majority of humanity as pure luxuries or at best pleasant childhood memories, unrelated to a responsible adult life. Society demands task and career orientation, and joy is left to your spare time. But even on your days off you seem to be too busy and have forgotten the true meaning and vital importance of happiness and joy. We, however, consider joy and happiness as skillful arts and a basic necessity for a fulfilling life. If you have not learned how to achieve this inner state of being, you will find yourself drowning in everyday duties and the consequent unhappiness.

Look at small children, the true masters of joy and happiness. Let them become your teachers. They find deep joy in the smallest things, such as watching a little insect making its way through a landscape of grass blades, observing sun rays sparkling through the leaves of a tree or indulging in the delicacy of ice cream. One of their secrets is that they live in the present moment. The sacred Now acts like a portal to your Higher Self.

We would like you to partake in an experiment. Dedicate an hour every day to the present moment, where you become aware of the sacredness of the Now. You will be surprised how even the most repetitive task such as cleaning can be completed with an ease never before experienced. After some practice you will feel joy arising seemingly out of the blue, for no apparent reason, for true joy is bound to neither reason nor cause. Joy is the smile of love arising when you are free and at peace. Joy has nothing to do with your life conditions. Joy arises from nowhere, enhancing your life with its magic. Joy is contagious. If you open your heart and live in the Now, you become receptive to joy and, because joy is contagious, it will affect others around you in the most beautiful way. Joy is the smile of God in your heart. It is the Divine's signature, letting you know that you are connected.

In your world, happiness and joy seem only to be linked to the good things that come to you and, if these 'good things' cease to occur, joy disappears. Yet, this is not real joy. Real joy and its sister happiness exist without reason. Real joy comes from an open heart, allowing you to see the beauty and tenderness of the world you live in and revealing the depth of the human soul. Joy and happiness arise when you see through the eyes of love. Joy is one way the Divine can meet you. If you open your heart wide enough, we will lend you our eyes and share the joy and beauty we perceive in everything — the love that pours from God's heart to yours. How wonderful will it be when you sense the peace and eternal bliss we feel. Our happiness and joy are not bound to outer circumstances. They are rather like the undercurrent of a river – always present, forever flowing.

Remember, being present in the Now is one of the keys to opening the sacred portal of your heart. Be in nature as often as you can, truly see, listen and activate all of your senses. Play with a child and be fully present. All of these activities can become an invitation to allow joy into your life. Even cleaning dirty dishes can provide you with an opportunity to explore joy when you are present in the Now. Meditation, dancing, singing, making love and celebrating your achievements in life are other opportunities to open up to joy. There are countless possibilities, often overlooked, to experience joy in being truly present to what is. We would like to invite you to be more creative in opening up to joy, so that joy can become your faithful companion.

Do you believe we are deadly serious as portrayed in many of your religious paintings? We can assure you we are not — we dance, love and smile. Love's movement is a silent smile: this is our dance. May you be inspired by our joy and follow its laughter home.

24

THE MISSING INNER CORE

We would like to shed light on a significant topic that is fundamental for your spiritual path. Examine with us how most religious institutions guided — or should we say misguided — humanity.

It all began after the enlightened teacher departed and his disciples assumed responsibility to pass on the teachings, or more precisely their interpretation of the teachings, to the greater public. In this way the message spread, and regrettably with it came increasing misunderstanding as the teachings travelled further from the original source. Much later in time, organised religions were established. Unfortunately, by this time fundamental errors of understanding already tainted the sacred teachings, thus preventing humanity from reaching inner liberation until today. The very foundation of every true spiritual path was and is love, peace and truth, including self-love.

We believe we have sufficiently explained in the previous chapters that you cannot become a match for your divine self if the frequency of your emotions and thoughts is incompatible with what you desire. This attitude can only result in blocking the very light you are longing for. Regrettably, this is what millions of spiritual seekers have experienced throughout history. These disciples followed their chosen religious paths wholeheartedly and with good intention, but, because the teachings were dismantled from their innermost core, which is love and self-love, they were unable to arrive at their destined goal. Later, some of the leaders of these religions even went so far as to turn this fundamental law into the opposite, declaring that self-love equals selfishness, an attribute that has to be avoided at any cost. What a sad irony when you consider that we, the enlightened Masters, gave you the keys to freedom, and religions, established in our names, turned these keys into physical, emotional and mental prison walls.

Dear ones, we see these prison walls falling and with them all false teachings. The true teachings will be set in place again, and all misguided beliefs will be eradicated. We will reveal Christ's original teachings and the message of all true Masters who have walked before and after him. To gain a more complete understanding of 'The Way', you first need to comprehend the consequences of the act of removing the innermost core of these teachings. The core is and was Love, which also means to love yourself and your brothers with all imperfections. Only through unconditional love is it possible to become a fitting match for your Higher Self and find inner peace and freedom.

The official Christian church doctrine gradually removed this essential foundation of the inner path and replaced it with the fear of being selfish. This led to agonising guilt when you considered your own needs and dared to care for yourself. In this way humanity was led astray for thousands of years — kept in the painful illusion of never being good enough. This soul-crippling belief spread like wildfire throughout all nations and religions. It is the most contagious and poisonous conviction, and you all still have it in common. As you know by now, we consider this false belief to be the root cause of the majority of your problems, causing preventable suffering and unhealthy emotional and mental contamination.

Let us turn our focus to history and examine more closely what has happened. As almost everyone was under the blinding spell of self-loathing, human mass consciousness became severely affected by this venom. No race or religion was spared; everyone was infected by the virus of emotional self-destruction and influenced by its lies, burying the truth for ages. Humanity began to believe in weakness and in their inability to connect to the Divine. As a consequence of this false conviction, saints and holy men were worshipped as being special human beings — the only ones able to find salvation. Few were capable of piercing through this blanket of lies and finding the way to their inner light. Instead of encouraging everyone to walk the path, the reports of the spiritual accomplishments of these holy men left the majority of the population once more convinced of their own insignificance — again, the divine light seemed unattainable and far away.

These extraordinary human beings, your saints, were often blackmailed and experienced torture in their lifetimes, and many lost their lives. Ironically, centuries later, some of them were put on pedestals as shining examples for the rest of humanity to admire. Others gained sainthood from the same church that persecuted them hundreds of years earlier. If we contemplate this alarming unfolding of events, the widening gap between the masses and the chosen few — the saints and holy men — becomes very obvious. Instead of spreading the message of these courageous souls — that everyone is able to unite with the Divine — which is the original teaching of Christ, Buddha and all other masters, the truth was again turned into its opposite. Once more, it was proclaimed that only 'chosen souls' are able to achieve union with the Divine. Do you realise how this has continued to repeat itself? The very few who broke through the manipulative control of the religious dogma walked 'The Way' and found the inner path; then were placed once more on an unreachable pedestal. Their achievements turned into exclusiveness, and again for the average person there was no salvation. So it is not surprising that you kept on believing in the ever-widening gap between you and God, where on one side you stand as sinners and on the other there are Christ, the saints and prophets — the Divine. Regrettably, this heritage of lies was passed on without question from one generation to the next for thousands of years. Few were able to see through this confusing mixture of truth, untruth and misinterpretation, except those who were in secrecy protecting the sacred teachings.

Now the time has come to uncover the truth in your temples, mosques, churches and synagogues and share it with everyone. God is not an exclusive God, who only reveals himself to priests, saints, prophets, gurus and spiritual teachers. God speaks to everyone in all languages through the heart. All of you are able to hear God's voice, when you listen to your heart. The voice of silence, however, can only be understood when you enter deep inner stillness. It is also impossible to walk the inner path without self-love, for it is the very foundation of any true spiritual development. How ridiculous is it to assume that God, declared by all religions as omnipotent, almighty, unconditional love, absolute truth and peace, would ask you not to love yourself.

We are aware that some might not like what we have to say, but we are neither interested in followers and admiration nor do we require your agreement. We simply state the truth and correct that which needs correction. We had to wait for this very moment, for never before in human history were so many of you longing for the truth and ready to listen. Remember, you always receive according to the frequency of your current thoughts and emotions. This is how it was, is and always will be. In truth your belief in fear was responsible for holding in place fear-based religions, with their false teachings. Your yearning for truth will bring about its long-awaited reappearance.

What do we mean by the term 'false teachings'? It is easy to understand when you consider that self-love, the core foundation of the spiritual path, gradually disappeared over time; and thus all teachings, originally meant as medicine for the soul, turned into poison for all who did not know how to love themselves. What can an individual who has not learned how to give to himself truly offer? True giving is to give without expectation, but someone who is unable to give to himself is in an energetic state of starvation and will have strong unconscious expectations towards others. If this person was to discover his own impure way of giving, self-judgment would be his predictable response. Yet what he needs is loving understanding towards his deprived aspect.

Let us use the metaphor of the cup that is overflowing and gives freely without expectations, for it is full — filled with love. Only from this stable and healthy inner foundation is a disciple able to walk the path of surrender and detachment, which is impossible for someone who has deprived himself of self-love. Everything this person will do is influenced by this lack of self-love. All actions, perceptions and insights will be tainted by this lack and are therefore impure. In this way the original teachings became false. Our offer is to assist you to first correct your own inner foundation. This is the only way to establish a strong base from which your inner path can develop clearly and with strength.

You might be irritated or even upset that we, who speak from the Heart of God, are harshly criticising religions. We only intend to correct the main errors in your spiritual teachings and do not wish to distress you more than necessary. We are aware that there are many loving individuals of goodwill and pure intent in your religious institutions. We do not judge them nor do we judge these institutions. We only wish to correct the misunderstandings in the teachings that have led you into the darkness of ignorance. Regrettably, these misinterpretations have set the perfect stage for the limiting belief in your separation from Source and successfully kept you in ignorance for thousands of years. It is now the time to open your eyes.

We do not even judge the ones who have intentionally put these false beliefs in place as tools for control and manipulation, for we are aware that one of your greatest fears is the fear of freedom and your own power. We understand the origin of this fear and are conscious of what it is capable of doing to you. This fear will even prevent the slightest possibility of freedom and inner power. The greatest human fear, however, is the fear of being loved. If you could see with our eyes — the eyes of the heart — you would realise that there is no reason for judgment. There are only more opportunities to be love and understand the truth of surrender. It is our love that we offer you with this transcription of truth.

25

THE SPIRITUAL EGO

We would like to talk about a relatively unknown, but from our perspective very common phenomenon that can be found inside established religious institutions as well as in various spiritual groups — the spiritual ego. We have observed that a large number of human beings are deeply longing for truth and salvation. Countless souls have already embarked on a dedicated spiritual journey and others are now preparing. We enjoy listening to the song of these souls. Without this song — your soul's melody — your inner journey can never commence. Unfortunately, many seekers are misguided by some spiritual teachers, for they are unaware of a particular form of misconduct that lays the foundation for abuse. We feel it is time to bring into the open the underlying cause of this unsatisfactory and damaging behaviour.

Some teachers have experienced a spiritual awakening and consequently believe themselves to be special or even enlightened. This is an error in thinking, for enlightenment can only be named a state of consciousness that is in permanent Oneness with the Divine. All stages leading to this consciousness of absolute inner freedom are only stepping stones to the actual goal. On the pathway to truth and Oneness, there are various obstacles to overcome, which will be explained separately in a dissertation of advanced teachings.

For now, we only wish to point out the illusion in which some spiritual teachers get trapped, for they teach about enlightenment without having personally reached that state of consciousness. You need to be aware that the spiritual ego has its own specific way of disguising itself. This can be compared with the mask created by your personal ego. Nonetheless, both forms of ego need correction, guidance and healing. The spiritual ego is complex in appearance, and demands a more thorough examination and greater vigilance.

It is hard to understand why you allow some spiritual teachers to get away with certain misconduct and indulgences, which you would harshly judge if the average person were to act so shamelessly. Let us use the example of a well-known guru who attracted numerous seekers and convinced them of his need to own a ridiculous number of Rolls Royces as appropriately fitting his spiritual concepts. Still, a fact that is far more damaging is that some teachers are using control and manipulation. Others are secretly sexually interfering with their students and some even abuse children. These teachers give explanations for their behaviour that portray their actions as being aligned with their spiritual doctrine, thus classifying their wrongdoings as entirely honourable.

We ask that you not only listen to a spiritual teacher but also observe his actions. Words without corresponding deeds are powerless. Some gurus use a mixture of different philosophies, ancient spirituality and psychology, which often only leads to confusion. In truth, they act the same way as religions have done for hundreds of years — manipulating and controlling their followers. We are aware of your hunger for truth, your longing for enlightenment. There is great joy concerning this long-awaited opening of your souls.

Yet we need to ask you to develop greater discernment. Understand that a true teacher neither wants your power nor needs your admiration. A true teacher of freedom will at all times direct your admiration to the Oneness, which is All That Is, the Source of all Creation, and never towards himself. A true teacher will hand you the tools to walk the path to freedom. He knows that your daily life provides you with all initiations necessary for reaching liberation. Most importantly, a true teacher has overcome his own spiritual ego, and so he is not misguided by it, unlike some self-appointed spiritual teachers.

We intentionally use the term 'self-appointed', for this is exactly what we mean. A true teacher of the inner path only walks into the public when called by the Divine and does not fall prey to the seduction of his spiritual ego. The temptations of the spiritual ego are similar to the deception of the personal ego: while they have different expressions, their intent is the same — their own survival. These wounded aspects require you to be someone important, someone special, someone above everyone else, someone who leads others and insists that only he can guide them. Look out for these attitudes in people. Be vigilant if someone wants to be your sole teacher or demands your obedience and money. He might have borrowed a few lines from the teachings of truth and may even practise some of them, but that does not make him a true teacher. Only the Divine can appoint a spiritual teacher. Observe carefully and listen to your heart. Your heart will always feel uneasy when words and deeds do not equate.

Are you aware that you do not actually need a spiritual teacher in a physical body to break free from your limitations? All of you have invisible teachers assigned to you according to your level of consciousness. These ascended beings are enlightened, free from the flaws of the spiritual ego and able to guide you to True Self-realisation. You only have to turn inwards and train with patience and perseverance in listening to your heart. Your sacred heart is the perfect spiritual guidance system and will never fail you.

We are not saying that there are no true spiritual teachers living on earth. In fact there are a number of extraordinary human beings, and it is well worth listening to their wisdom and inspiration. You can be assured that these teachers want neither your power nor your money. These souls will have no interest in control, manipulation or any form of dependency. We call these beings living Masters. They are rare — rarer than you might believe.

We ask you to develop discernment, independence and strength. Some of you might even need a few encounters with abusive spiritual teachers and gurus. In the end, these experiences will serve you as a profound learning opportunity in the art of discernment. In this instance, through the painful insight that all you gained was dependency — not the promised freedom — you will come to the realisation that a long journey still awaits you to find your true nature. So ultimately everything, even the spiritual ego, serves the light.

In this context, we would like to bring to your attention another law: 'The Darkness Serves the Light.' You might be surprised to hear this, for it seems to contradict everything that you have been taught and led to believe. Nevertheless, this is the truth. The darkness provides you with the obstacles for your inner growth. In overcoming these hurdles you will gain deep insights, and the darkness will have lost its power over you, at least in relation to this particular aspect.

Beloveds, a soul should only ever surrender to the Divine. Any other form of surrender is pointless, even dangerous, and a long road of recovery awaits those who give their power away. This applies not only to priests, gurus and spiritual teachers, but also to therapists and doctors as well as anyone else who inspires you and you admire. The only way to safely surrender is to surrender to the Divine, which can only be achieved in the sanctuary of inner stillness. This is sacred business between God and you. It has been like this since the beginning of time. The Divine has no spiritual ego, will neither abuse you nor manipulate or control you. The only intention of the Divine is to assist you in your return from a long illusionary journey where you were dreaming of separation.

The Divine loves you. Unlike certain gurus, God does not offer exclusive retreats, where talks are only granted at special times and personal audiences are rare. The Divine is always there for you, ready to listen day and night, all of your life. God is teaching you through your everyday life. You are the ones who need to lift your feet of clay and open your hearts. The purpose of this book is to provide you with the necessary instructions. This will require all of your attention. Yet you will not have to leave your life behind or retreat to a monastery to reach inner freedom. You will, however, have to leave your old ways behind. This means how you currently perceive life, yourself, others and God. You will have to go into your 'inner monastery'. In the sacred space of your heart you will find your silent retreat. There you will learn to listen and be able to hear the voice of silence. Each time you follow the guidance of the Divine, this voice of stillness will become clearer, louder and easier to understand. Then life will test you, if you truly walk the path of the heart. As we have said, words without corresponding actions have no meaning and thus no power. These words of wisdom do not belong to you; they belong to those who have found the truth.

'The Way' is less mystical than you might imagine. It is all about your courage to live life in integrity with your heart. Your spiritual heart is the place where you can always reach us. In your heart, you and the Heart of God are connected. It is necessary for the ones who feel a calling to teach to first establish an intimate and stable connection with the Divine. Carefully examine if there are any traits of your spiritual ego trying to seduce you into self-importance. When you find them, trace them back to their origin and you will recognise that they always derive from your personal ego. It might be an overlooked wound that simply needs your love. Realise there is nothing to fight, not even the spiritual ego. There is only more to love. We ask you to develop spiritual discernment, naked honesty, courage and integrity, in order to live in harmony with your originating spirit — *Love*.

26

THE RIGHT USE OF POWER

Let us review the close connection between power and corruption and how this all to common abuse of power can be prevented. The answer is as simple as it is profound — through enlightenment. Enlightenment — the complete realignment with Source and embodiment of our divine nature is the only way to avoid power, money, fame and wealth corrupting your soul. Only when human beings are one with their true essence are they able to successfully deal with these challenges.

We have discussed in the previous chapter that some spiritual teachers experience another form of corruption — the interference of their spiritual ego. History provides you with countless examples of political and religious leaders who were compromised by worldly power and wealth. In actual fact no human being is able to deal appropriately with such a degree of power without previously having undergone deep spiritual cleansing and training. Any attempt to do so is a near impossible endeavour and destined to fail. We see this practice of ignorance soon disappearing from earth, for it does not serve your highest good.

In the near future, your leaders will have to undergo thorough spiritual training and initiations. Only students who have reached the highest level of wisdom, inner discipline, love and compassion will pass these tests. In addition to the required psychological and spiritual abilities, they will have to develop exceptional leadership and professional skills to gain the right to stand for election in your country. It has once been like this on earth, even though those times passed long ago. Legends from the ancient court of King Arthur tell of these noble men and women and their attempts to bring about a kingdom of love, peace and truth. Similar stories can be found in all cultures and will once again become your future guideline.

Today, a substantial part of humanity has a deep yearning for wise leadership. Hopes and dreams of a better, fairer and more peaceful world are projected on a potential or elected leader. Yet even when a man of goodwill and integrity enters the world stage, we observe that his hands are still bound by forces literally working in the shadows behind the scenes. These men believe in the illusion of their own omnipotence because of the control and manipulation they have exerted for so long. However, their power is waning and will soon cease to exist, for the divine light is overtaking government on earth.

The Children of the Sun are returning to take on the rulership of this planet. The precious souls of enlightened Masters are incarnating at this time to expose the truth and re-educate humanity as to their true purpose and the meaning of life. They are providing you with the tools for living life in peace, love and truth. When you follow the advice of these enlightened beings you will live in peace with one another. Day by day the frequency of the light is increasing on earth and these souls are being secretly prepared in the ancient ways for their roles as leaders. They have passed serious spiritual initiations — Source itself is providing them with all the necessary preparation for the difficult task of dealing with worldly and spiritual power, as well as the privileges and temptations arising from possessing great wealth. In order that they may truly serve, their training has spanned many lifetimes, including this life. If you are attentive, you can already see them emerging. Although their appearances are rare at present, they stand as shining lights among the corrupt, immature and unconscious who have been set in place by the darkness. These dark forces literally work in the shadows and use elected leaders as public puppets to divert attention from their own secret goals. Yet you will soon see the living examples of integrity appearing more often in the public eye. There will come a time when humanity will realise that only people who have passed a thorough spiritual training can become their leader. It will be customary that your leaders have to possess a range of exceptional personal, professional and spiritual skills in order to stand for election. Only then will they be equipped to guide you into a prosperous future. These leaders will appear when humanity is ready and 'energetically' calls for them.

We observe that the vast majority of humanity is no longer idealising war. There are only a few misguided souls left who drive the 'war machine'. Most of you long for a peaceful world and leaders acting from inner wisdom. As you know, you are creating your world according to the law of attraction, and it will be your longing that attracts these new leaders to appear. If you would be at peace and envisage a world of peace instead of worrying about a world plagued by war and corruption, peace would consequently come — it has to come. It is time to realise that your collective human consciousness is calling the world into manifestation. This is the very reason why we are so interested in raising your consciousness and particularly that of your leaders. This is the only way to create a better world. Can you see the active part you need to play? You can change the world significantly by letting go of your worries and negative judgments. We do not mean to become blind, naive or indifferent towards the negative events unfolding on earth; we do however ask that you stop wasting your precious energy with fruitless complaints. Instead, we invite you to visualise the world you would like to see and actively build on it. The first step towards this goal is to imagine the world you want to see and focus on this vision as often as you can. You can practise this visualisation while occupied with mundane tasks such as driving the car, gardening or ironing your clothes. Imagine your dream for this world and feel it, as if it is already happening.

Power belongs to the Enlightened Ones. They are the ones who seek neither power nor acknowledgment. They do not need attention, but are capable of handling attention with humility and dignity. Yet we have not arrived at this point. What you are witnessing at the moment is the dying of the old system based on control and fear. Simultaneously, the initial signs of a new world are emerging with a different set of rules — in alignment with the divine laws. You are presently experiencing the transition from one way of life to another. Patience and positive focus are the requirements to withstand the phasing out of the old ways of fear. Look at the promising developments in the world and within yourself, rising like young sprouts in springtime. Give the blossoming of this new consciousness your undivided attention and love. If you were to show the same regard and care for your inner wounds, you would pass through this global and personal transformation without unnecessary confusion and inner turmoil. In this context it is useful to remember that the world is nothing but a reflection of your own consciousness. The old system, built on fear, control and manipulation, is fading fast. Souls who continue to hang on to the old oppressive system need time for rethinking and inner healing. Unfortunately, the healing process for most of these reluctant souls will occur on the other side of the veil, after they have passed the transition of death.

Parallel to this inner and outer remodelling, the promised New Age is descending and is already revealing its powerful influence in many areas of life. You only need to look at the recent developments in medicine, science, environmental care and psychology, where significant breakthroughs in holistic thinking have taken place. Observe all areas of life and you will realise how many promising changes have already emerged, which only a few decades ago would have been unthinkable. These are the messengers of the new time.

The New Earth can only manifest if as many of you as possible understand the urgency of raising your consciousness. Begin with the basic spiritual teachings and apply these laws in your daily life. Your change in consciousness will be reflected in your governments and its leaders. In the not too distant future we might see the dream of King Arthur and the Knights of the Round Table come true. In the most unexpected ways, his spirit and the spirit of his knights will return to earth, fulfilling the promise they once gave to themselves and the world. They will complete the task that they were unable to accomplish over a thousand years ago.

Many others who turned the wheel of history are returning with them to assist you and gracious Mother Gaia in this exciting transformation to a new form of society. These awakened men and women hold the keys to your journey to freedom. Know that your spiritual awakening is the main purpose of your life. All of the great ones in history knew this secret. Let us mention some of the great initiates: Jesus, Mary Magdalene, Buddha, Mohammed, Zoroaster, Krishna, Moses, Akhenaten, Leonardo da Vinci, Albert Einstein,

Benjamin Franklin, Abraham Lincoln, Jean d'Arc, St Francis, Lao Tzu, Hatshepsut, Mahatma Gandhi, Comte de Saint Germain, Johann Wolfgang Goethe and countless more.

Interestingly, all of these extraordinary human beings, who are still greatly honoured today, had one thing in common: they walked the path of initiation. Their knowledge, wisdom and genius were derived from their spiritual connection and inner work. They only became exceptional human beings because of their connection with the Divine. Their lives serve as an invitation to follow their example. Begin with your own journey to one day stand in line with these leaders of humanity as one of them. Not for the sake of your name being remembered — it is simply about you becoming a full expression of your highest potential and learning to deal wisely with power if destiny presents it to you.

27

RE-PARENTING THE EGO

Let us examine the true meaning of the term 'ego' and the deeper origin of this often carelessly used word. The ego is the part of you that fears and hopes, likes, dislikes, judges and carries your conditioning. It is the aspect of your personality that has not yet received complete healing. This is the reason why the ego behaves in ways that most of you judge and despise when you discover its traits in your own or someone else's character. We consider judgment and any form of inner fight, whether directed towards oneself or others, to be entirely useless and destructive. We would like to explain why we do not hold in high regard this common behaviour that infests your society and almost all spiritual teachings.

Religions and the majority of spiritual groups fight in unison against 'the ego', portraying it as being almost demonic. This is a distortion of the truth. Everything you fight against will only become stronger through the focus and energy you give to it — even if you believe your fight is justified. The ego only acts in a selfish, self-centred and ruthless manner because it represents your unhealed aspects. The ego is nothing you can fight against; instead it needs to be acknowledged as your wounded and misguided part, crying out for love and guidance. Only in this way will real transformation occur. Most of your spiritual and religious groups have not yet realised that the condemnation of 'the ego' is a misconception and one of the most profound errors in their teachings. The sad results of this misunderstanding are suffering and the significant stagnation of your inner development.

As with everything that is misaligned with love and truth, your ego needs healing. You are the only one who can do this for yourself. These wounded parts — mistaken by your flawed conditioned belief as 'ruthless ego' — can only be integrated if your human and divine self re-educate and re-parent them. Living an ascetic life — one of condemnation or rigorous fight against 'the ego' — will never lead to a resolution of this problematic aspect and its reintegration. This is an unattainable endeavour, for integration can only occur through love, to unify that which is apparently separate and therefore not whole. Fight, on the other hand, always implies division and further separation. Do you realise how the attitude of fight is opposing the process of integration? It is impossible to achieve union with the Divine while rigorously fighting against your ego. Students of different religious denominations have tried to achieve union with God in this way for thousands of years and failed. God is a God of love, truth and peace. How can fight ever serve God?

In order to come closer to God you need to become more loving, more peaceful and more truthful with yourself and your fellow humans. This is the only way to succeed. To be truthful means to have an honest look at yourself and identify where you are not loving, not fair, at war, greedy, jealous or angry. Simply acknowledge these emotions without judgment, become aware of their presence and recognise the havoc they create in your life. Then make a commitment to transformation and healing.

Begin with the aspect you consider to be your most unpleasant and call it forth in your meditations or visualisations. Ask this part what it needs, and with perseverance and practice you will receive an answer. Then act in accordance with what you have received and give love and understanding to this wounded part. After a while you will realise that this aspect, previously considered to be your worst, will begin to soften, and you will feel an unknown inner peace and relaxation. You will sense a shift happening, subtle at first, until the moment arises when you observe the wound closing. Then turn your attention to the next aspect of your negative ego and apply the same healing technique until only love is left. Love is the great healer. Every demon that fear has created, as well as any negative character trait, can be transformed into the light with love. There is nothing mysterious about this process: everyone can apply it and harvest positive results.

It is concerning that many seekers get lost in the sheer abundance of 'spiritual knowledge', which they accumulate like a shopaholic without proper application to their daily lives. Do you realise that this behaviour leads you nowhere and only leaves you confused? We therefore keep our conversation as simple as possible to prevent further temptation, which would only fuel pointless mind acrobatics. We prefer that you learn one subject and truly master it, rather than apparently know so much and live so little.

Review the way you treat your unhealed aspects that birthed 'the ego' and transform these attitudes. With this small but significant change you will be able to experience tremendous healing and a quantum leap in consciousness. Know that we love you. Did one of us not say 'Love thy neighbour as thyself'? The first part of this verse is still found as a remnant in the form of charity in your churches, whereas the last part seems almost entirely forgotten. It is time to remember the whole sentence, for only then does it truly make sense. You cannot love your brother if you do not love all that you are, including your ego.

To prevent future misunderstanding, we would like to clarify that we do not support you in allowing your ego to get away with negative behaviour or defending egoism with the blunt statement 'I love myself'. This is certainly not the purpose of these teachings of love. What we are saying is that you need to re-educate and re-parent that which is lost, abandoned and unhealed in you to be able to reintegrate these parts into your greater self. Without a 'healed ego' you cannot return home and heaven's door will appear closed to you.

Only if you take your ego by the hand, as did Parzival with his dark brother Feirefiz, will you be shown the Holy Grail and heaven will embrace you with all its glory. Feirefiz stands as a metaphor for the shadow part, which becomes the transformed ego. Parzival represents your transformed human part in alignment with the divine self, taking your ego firmly but lovingly by the hand to guide it home. Unless you adopt the notion of harmlessness towards yourself and all sentient beings, you will remain unable to experience lasting inner and outer peace. There is nothing to fight against, only more to love!

28

SOUL PURPOSE

Dear ones, we would like to look at a question that frequently arises in your hearts when you have embarked on your spiritual journey: 'What is my soul purpose?' Many of you feel helpless regarding the answer to this burning question. Some even lose their sense of direction when they are unable to find a satisfying answer. The answer is the same for everyone. Your soul purpose is to remember who you are and awaken to your divine nature. How you perceive your soul purpose will, however, change according to the continuous transformation of your consciousness. Everything changes as consciousness evolves.

For a better understanding let us use the analogy of climbing a mountain. Imagine that you are halfway to the top, look around and take in everything you see from this position. Then climb for another two hours and again absorb with all your senses what is presented to you. You will perceive different surroundings to those you enjoyed a short while ago. It is still the same mountain, only your point of reference has changed. Now, imagine you are at the top of the mountain and the full view surrounds you. A breathtaking scene of deep valleys and towering mountains unfolds before your eyes, very different when compared to the previous sights. Yet it is still the same mountain, only another perspective.

The same applies to your perceptions as you walk through life — they are forever changing according to the shifts in your consciousness. For instance, when you feel rather depressed the outlook you have on life and your ability to cope are narrowed, altered and limited by the dark filter of negative thoughts. Alternatively, when you are in high spirits you feel that you can conquer the world and your motto seems to be, 'The sky is the limit'. This is a simple example that every human being knows from their own experience — it is the same person, the same life, but the change in consciousness creates a vastly different perspective on life.

Let us now focus on the search for your life mission. The true task of all human beings is to awaken, align with their divine self and one day become enlightened or self-realised. Enlightenment means the stable, indestructible, permanent connection to your Higher Self and its embodiment, maintained under all circumstances. The path to this noble goal is as individual as you all are. What you perceive as your soul purpose or your true mission will naturally change. As you pass through one challenge you will soon be presented with the next.

It is unfortunate that many spiritual seekers have become almost obsessed with the quest for their soul purpose. When we look into your hearts, we often find a deep longing for an extraordinary mission, such as 'saving the world'. We also see in some of you the desire to be someone important, someone with great psychic abilities or a successful healer, writer or public speaker or similar. You wish to be someone you are not at this very moment. This is exactly our point, for the question you so frequently ask is based on the flawed belief that your current life situation is unsatisfactory and you are not good enough. From this foundation of lack you cannot find an answer.

Your questions arise from fear, causing only further lack. How can you find a positive and soul-fulfilling answer from a fear-based negative foundation? It is impossible. You need to ask the right question. Does this remind you of the old tales where the student of life, entering the path of initiation, is asked to carefully consider his question? You may remember the medieval tale of Parzival, who stood in front of the Grail King Anfortas unable to ask the right question and as a consequence had to leave to continue his quest for the Holy Grail. A fear-based question cannot provide you with a positive answer. This is why we suggest that you first heal your fear before asking this vital question. Only from a place of self-love can you truly begin to ponder this question. Then enter the stillness of your sacred heart and bring forth the quest for your soul purpose to your divine self and spiritual guides.

Some of you may have had a specific task assigned long before incarnating, requiring greater service for humanity than others. Do not, however, compare yourself with someone else. A person whose name becomes known or even famous is of no higher value than someone who silently assumes his inner work and remains unknown to the world. It is about you doing what you love, for this is where you will shine. Always follow your heart — let this be your guidance. Prefer to go slow and steady, rather than run too fast, for few have the capability of dealing with the consequences that arise from speed.

Do what you do as best you can with all your heart and soul. When you have mastered a particular lesson, you will be presented with the next challenge.

Your main mission on earth is to love yourself unconditionally, to dissolve all fear and to become a true expression of your humanness as well as your divinity. This way you will build the sacred 'Rainbow Bridge' between heaven and earth and so bring heaven to earth.

When you follow your heart you need to be ready to take risks. Prepare yourself to trust the unknown, without becoming naive. Do whatever you can to ease the burden of the ones who suffer hardship. Do whatever your heart is whispering to you — follow its call. Remember, every great enterprise started in a small way. Believe in your mission regardless of all setbacks and difficulties, remain focused on the goal, continue to walk towards it and you will succeed. Everything you do, no matter how great or small it may appear, is measured in a different way in heaven. We only see your intention, the love, truth and peace you radiate when you do what you do — or the lack of it.

Dear ones, when the question arises again in you, 'What is my soul purpose', do not expect to be 'a hero who is saving the world' too soon. This world has to be saved by more than one hero. It needs all of you, each one of you!

Become still and ask yourself the following questions:

1. Am I true to myself in the way I live my life?
2. Do I treat myself and my fellow humans with love and respect?
3. What do I long for in this world?
4. What is my dream for my life?
5. What do I love the most?
6. What is it that I am good at?
7. How can I best serve my own awakening and humanity?

If you truthfully answer these questions you will find directions guiding you towards your soul purpose.

A soul purpose can look as different as you are all different. Someone might have lived his hero and saint aspect — even his leader and king part — in previous lives, and feels that this life is about learning to be present to see his children grow up and have an active part in their upbringing. Another soul might have acted in ways that she is now regretting, such as abusing her power, and this time wishes to demonstrate that she is able to use power wisely and becomes a well-known healer or spiritual teacher. Never judge anyone by outer appearances, for human eyes cannot see. We always see the whole storyline, whereas you only perceive a small part of it. Only the eyes of the heart are able to look at the greater picture. Truth will reveal itself to the ones who walk the path of initiation and live in surrender to the Divine.

Your soul purpose is to be the best 'you' you can be — where you are, right at this moment, in this place, with exactly the people that surround you. Be the most loving, truthful and peaceful you can be to yourself and others. If there is a special mission for you, we assure you that we have our ways to make this known. You cannot silence the call of your soul or your Creator. We wish to remind you that no life is insignificant in contributing to the light on earth. It is all about your heart and how you do things, not what you do. Follow your heart, live your dreams, be love and be present with what is.

29

THE MIND

The human mind is an expression of the mental body. It was originally created to be as calm as a still lake on a warm summer's night, simply reflecting the light of the moon with no wind swirling its surface. A peaceful mirror image of what *is*. The mind only engaged when its active role was required. Unfortunately, few on your planet are able to use their minds in this way. You have forgotten the actual purpose of the mind and become entirely lost in the havoc it plays out in your daily lives. Today the human mind is rarely ever still or, metaphorically speaking, your lake is unable to truly reflect what *is*, for it is in constant uproar. Your mind resembles a thunderstorm, trying to deal with the thousands of thoughts flooding through it, consciously and unconsciously. There is no stillness to be found there. How did it come to this?

We observe that the mind is worshipped on your planet. The more the mind is able to fill itself and download information at any given time, the more 'intelligent' someone appears and therefore the more honoured and valued. Intelligence seems to be one of the most desirable attributes of your society. We are in disbelief at the naivety of this assessment and believe you have mistaken intelligence for the freedom from ignorance, which indeed is truly desirable. The significant difference between intelligence and true inner freedom, however, is that intelligence can function on its own without the vital connection to the heart, whereas freedom from ignorance can only be achieved through the surrender to the heart. In fact, through the connection to your sacred heart you are able to access a higher form of intelligence — the universal mind.

We believe you overrate intelligence in the same way as you do the mind. The mind was originally set in place to be the servant of the heart and your heart is the sacred connection to your Higher Self — to the Divine. Sadly, most human beings closed their hearts, disconnected from their true nature and the mind became a poor substitute for their spiritual heart. The 'servant' now sits on the throne and tries its best to govern, but as you can clearly see, it is not well equipped for the complexity of rulership, regardless of how intelligent it may appear. Intelligence without the connection to the heart and Higher Self is neither able to free you from ignorance nor provide you with true wisdom. Intelligence is simply a wonderful ability that needs to be guided by love through your spiritual heart.

Your mind is trying its best to understand the complexities and contradictions of life. If presented with a problem, it attempts to find solutions through using its ability to think. It endeavours to make sense of a world in confusion with ever-mounting challenges. Yet true understanding can only arise when your heart is engaged, allowing you to see through the eyes of your soul. This is how your soul whispers to you, making you aware of the invisible learning opportunities presented by your outer circumstances.

The mind is supposed to be the servant of your soul. It is extremely useful and functions well if you have to organise your day or are in need of order and structure — for instance, to research the political background of a certain event, prepare your taxes or perform similar tasks. Yet this is not the only way humanity uses the mind. You use it to solve delicate relationship matters, comprehend the deeper meaning of spiritual beliefs and try to make sense of a fast-changing world nearing collapse. Many can no longer cope with the flood of information engulfing you and the planet. Consequently, your mind becomes overwhelmed and you feel a sense of powerlessness leading to a cycle of compulsive thinking.

Complex situations that humanity as well as you individually are facing need to be contemplated in great inner stillness to find resolutions. You must therefore learn how to still the mind. If you wish to have a contented, peaceful and successful life, the mind needs to be placed under the rulership of the heart — otherwise it is impossible for the mind to access the wisdom of the soul. Intelligence in itself only leads to an accumulation of knowledge when not guided by your heart. Where did some of your intelligent leaders who lacked true wisdom and love lead their nations? Into war and disaster. We do not disregard intelligence, for the ability to think, even think the impossible, is one of the necessary foundations for freeing yourself and changing the world. Yet your emotions must first be healed before your thinking can be freed.

Dear ones, to solve your current problems your worship of the mind has to cease. The mind needs to be replaced with the rulership of the heart, where all wisdom and the treasures of your soul lie dormant, but ready to be accessed. Every question a human being can ever possibly ask is already answered in this very place. You simply need to learn how to find your way to your inner sanctum. Meditate, seek silence and turn inwards whenever possible. Valuable tools to still your mind are the practice of tai chi, chi gong, yoga, living in the *now* as well as different forms of breathing techniques, meditation, prayers, affirmations and mantras or simply being in nature. Become still like the calm surface of a lake, reflecting only the beauty of the sun and moon.

Most of you, however, are too busy with thinking to even recognise the sun and moon and miss the answers to your burning questions. The mind is meant to be a tool for your soul and Higher Self and has to accept its rightful place. It has to understand that it is not the director, rather the servant of your life. The shift from mind consciousness to heart consciousness is not easy, yet it is crucial, and it requires discipline, perseverance, patience and vigilance.

To successfully accomplish this replacement, you have to become the observer. Watch yourself and note how many times a day you allow your mind to run wild. Call it back, calm it down, breathe deeply and focus on your breath. Go into meditation and re-centre yourself by opening your heart. A lot of the effort that you are exerting stems from the overuse of your mind as it desperately tries to find resolutions that would come to you with ease if you turned to the wisdom of your heart. We see that, in the future, relaxation techniques, meditation and certain forms of martial arts will be taught from an early age to the children of the New World. These fortunate souls will know the proper use of the mind from the beginning.

You need to reprogram your mind so that it can become useful again. This valuable tool cannot be in constant use. Even a machine needs rest. Your mind never rests and even seems to follow you into your dreams. Your true potential can only be discovered if you begin to train your mind while simultaneously developing an open heart. Only then will humanity discover that what it believed was possible was only a very limited part of what it is truly capable of achieving.

Your journey to become a 'hu-man', a divine man, will then begin.

Your mind as it is now used only acts as an obstacle for your Higher Self and soul along with your unbalanced emotions. Unhealed emotions contract the emotional body and make its appearance dense and dark, and in some cases even create holes. The noise of undirected random thoughts pollutes your mental body and acts as a barrier towards your spiritual body, cutting you off from your greater self. The mind needs to be stilled, disciplined and cleared. When the mastery of the mind is accomplished, you are able to focus on a particular thought to deliberately create what you desire and so give the required mental energy for its manifestation. Regrettably the way you use mental energy at the moment is reflected by the chaos in your world. A true Master only uses the tool of his mind when needed. His thoughts are then focused like a laser beam on the desired outcome of his chosen creation.

The longer you think and feel a thought, the stronger and faster it will manifest in your physical world. We talked before about each of you creating your own world. To create a world that is not just the result of random thoughts, fed by vague hopes and fears, you need to master your mind. Give your thoughts your full attention. Your thoughts can be compared with a bow pointing at the target and the emotion relating to this particular thought is the arrow. When the arrow is aligned with your bow, which in turn is in alignment with your goal, nothing can prevent your desire from becoming reality. Having your emotions in alignment or resistance to your thoughts will determine whether or not you reach your goal.

In order to become a conscious co-creator and master of your reality you need to practise this skilful art. We invite you to embark on the journey of mastership, which will lead you from the confusion of your noisy mind to deep clarity and true inner peace, a place where your mind will serve your soul. You will then build a wonderful life for yourself as well as for the whole world, for the enlightened mind is able to create miracles and thus serve its original purpose.

When you fully surrender and embody Christ consciousness, inner peace will unfold and your mind will experience stillness and emptiness, beyond human imagination. Whenever you need to know an answer or make a decision, the Divine will provide you with the required knowledge in gracious abundance. Unnecessary planning and compulsive thinking will simply fall away, for you will live in the eternal Now. The pathway to a miraculous life will have finally opened.

30

PEACE BETWEEN OPPOSING ASPECTS

Let us examine the opposing inner aspects of a human being that cause unnecessary internal tension and inner fight. For instance, take the part of you that likes to enjoy, celebrate, party and on the other hand the perfectionist aspect that wants to continually do the right thing. You all have these opposing parts within you, regardless of how long you walked your spiritual path. The only difference is that the journey of the beginner is often marked by the denial of these opposing aspects, engaging in an inner war, whereas the more experienced student shows a greater awareness towards his various different inner aspects and in this example — his controlling and disciplined aspect, contrary to his adventurous part.

Few of you have made peace with these conflicting facets and truly integrated them. Even the more advanced students often display ambivalence and judgment towards their opposing inner sides. Only when you have truly reached inner freedom are you able to experience lasting peace and a constructive coexistence between these energies. How can this desirable state of being be achieved? You may look at the *Tao Te Ching* of Lao Tzu for advice and gain insight into the wisdom of this ancient teaching where Lao Tzu talks of 'the middle path' and true inner balance. This will be our subject for this chapter.

Dear ones, many different aspects live within all of you, but for now we wish to focus on the parts we have just mentioned. In most of you two sides oppose each other to a degree that there appears to be no common denominator. When you find two of your aspects in opposition to such an extent, your subsequent judgment indicates how much you are out of alignment in this area. This should be no reason for great concern; rather an invitation to bring these opposing inner voices together. Call them to sit at one table to begin the long-needed conversation. Imagine: it would be like inviting Jimmy Hendrix and a monk to talk about what direction to choose in life — your life. This is how impossible it will feel in the beginning, when your conflicting aspects begin their conversation. Be courageous and do it anyway. Let each of them have their say, honour them, give them your full attention and listen carefully with the respect they deserve, for each is a part of you. They need you to finally become aware of their existence, to suppress or deny them no longer.

Depending on your mood and level of awareness, you might lend your ear to 'Jimmy' and on other occasions be more open to listen to 'the monk', forgetting it was not so long ago that you had entirely identified with your 'Jimmy Hendrix aspect'. You are neither the monk nor Jimmy Hendrix: these are only two of your unhealed sides directing you, for they have not yet found peace. How can they ever find peace if you remain unaware of their existence? You are the only one who is able to support these aspects, learn from each other and find true inner peace and balance. One day they will walk 'the middle path' and assist you to become 'the living Tao'. Again, it is you who needs the courage to take responsibility, walk into the unknown and become a true student of life. Welcome, friends, to the sacred mystery school life itself presents! This is the true journey home, to the consciousness where no pretence exists.

We see many spiritual seekers living in pretence and are aware it is not their ill intent that led to this behaviour. Rather, this unfortunate conduct developed from the ignorance of the reality of their inner aspects and how to heal them. We raise this subject to encourage more honesty, which is vital for your path to freedom. We do not need new saints. You simply need to understand that when all aspects are loved and integrated you will be truly alive and contribute to the abundance of love, truth and peace on earth. You will become a vessel for your Higher Self, which will live through you and gift you with divine knowledge and wisdom beyond your wildest dreams.

For this to become your reality, you need to end all pretence such as hiding behind the monk as a convenient comfort zone. The aspect of the monk has its valuable purpose, as does your 'wild side'. You need to recognise both as important parts of your inner life. Invite them to communicate, so that they may learn from one another in the most unexpected ways. They equally have their point of view and right to live. Their antagonism only shows their imbalance, yet they need one another, their opposite, to achieve true inner balance. Have courage and bring them into your heart. Take time and space, listen with great awareness to what they have to share. You might be surprised what they may teach. Regrettably, the majority of human beings are unaware of their various inner aspects. They can, however, be studied in detail in psychology books under the heading 'archetypes'.

We have now introduced you to the reality that you have a variety of inner aspects, contrary to the belief that there is one homogeneous 'I'. We wish to continue our conversation on this foundation. These opposing and imbalanced aspects are split-off parts of your whole being, and periodically create havoc in your life. It is time to listen and understand these apparent enemies. We have chosen these two aspects as an example to highlight a common invisible inner fight. You can choose any of your opposing parts and apply the above-mentioned healing conversation. All of these aspects need your love, understanding and willingness to take full responsibility to integrate them. Only then will you be able to merge with your divine self, for every condemned, judged and abandoned aspect will hinder and hold you back on your spiritual journey.

You can see the ugly face of denial and misunderstanding of these inner sides of human nature in the recent history of the Catholic Church, with the rising number of child abuse cases involving the priesthood. These priests try as best as they can to live the aspect of the monk and in doing so completely suppress their other facets, including their sexuality and sensuality. If they did not have to deny these aspects of human nature, and were allowed to enjoy the pleasure of sexuality, child abuse would not exist to this horrendous extent.

Realise that every aspect of life requires balance. When you go too far to one end of the scale, nature has its own way of balancing by taking you the same distance to the opposite side. Denial and oppression towards your inner aspects are always reflected in your outer world. We would love to see more honesty. Let the monk in you learn from your primal part how to relax, enjoy life and go with the flow. This is the lesson from your Jimmy Hendrix aspect. Jimmy can then learn from the monk that partying does not have to lead to excess and unpleasant side effects. Let your Jimmy live and he may no longer need to drink excessively and stay up all night. Decipher these messages from your unhealed archetypes that are calling you to raise your awareness that your life is out of balance.

Give credit to all sides of you, for they are your teachers. As you do so, these parts will then feel seen and valued and be able to heal — eventually to become your advisers, leading you to a more wholesome life. Thank and invite them to a gathering, where both can be present without fight and thus become aware of their respective rights to live. Learn from them and watch them grow. In time, you will observe the monk losing his rigidity and stiffness, getting into the flow of life and opening up to joy. Furthermore, he will have less judgment towards himself and others and develop a deeper understanding of his own shortcomings and those of humanity, to a point where he can truly love all and everything that is. Is this not what the monk was searching for in the first place when he embarked on his spiritual path? In the end it is Jimmy who teaches him an important lesson, the lesson of tolerance and love. This lesson gives him the key to heaven, for it shows how to become love — to be love — for the Divine is love.

On the other hand, Jimmy will learn discipline from the monk without spoiling the fun of the party. In the end Jimmy and the monk will become friends and will often celebrate life together. A time will come when there is only Oneness left. When all your aspects are in love with one another, you have achieved a major step on your inner journey and your heart will be filled with deep gratitude. Have the courage to invite your most opposing parts to the sacred inner table, so that they may learn from one another. These forgotten inner opponents will help you to gain wisdom and the necessary inner balance to become truly whole. May peace be with you.

31

THE PHYSICAL BODY

Let us talk about your physical body and how to treat it the right way. Western society appears to be obsessed with physical appearance, youthfulness and beauty, pretending to have genuine interest in the physical body, your vehicle on earth. We intentionally use the word 'pretend', for we observe neither real interest nor a true understanding of the body. Instead, we see a rather forceful attitude towards it, attempting to create an illusionary mask of perfection, similar to the inner mask built on the emotional level. Unfortunately, your focus on the physical level is again pointed in the wrong direction. All attention is concentrated on the outside and not within, where it is needed, to create true beauty and long-lasting health. We will place the Spiral, the ancient symbol of creation, the symbol of the Goddess and the Mother, onto this subject to bring light.

Dear ones, your human body needs to be built from the inside out, to be able to express true beauty and strength. An unloved body — cared for inappropriately, draped in the latest fashionable clothes, decorated with makeup and the latest hairstyle — can only pretend to be beautiful and in good health for a short while. We believe you need to review the information already available to humanity to gain a real understanding of what health and beauty truly require. Here is a brief overview of the key aspects that are relevant to your health and wellbeing.

Exercise

In order to be vital and fit, your body needs movement every day. This is how it was designed. Choose movement you enjoy, that is not forced and practised reluctantly, for only if you enjoy your exercise will it become a regular part of your life.

Food

Your body needs natural unprocessed food in the right balance. There are more than enough books available for everyone to find their own way of enjoying healthy, wholesome and delicious food.

Water

You need at least 2 litres of pure and clean water each day, to replenish all of your cells and transport waste and toxins from your body. The most expensive creams, facials and other beauty treatments cannot replace the benefits of drinking water, cleansing your skin from within and freeing the physical body of toxins.

Immerse your body in water. Water is not only an element that cleans the surface of your physical body, it also balances and clears all of your subtle energy fields. Use your imagination. Lie in a bath or have a shower, visualise the water as pure white light surrounding you. Ask this light to purify your aura field and release all unwanted, negative and used energies. Everyone will agree with the necessity of cleaning your body every day, but few know of the extraordinary benefits of a cleansing ritual to balance your emotional, mental and spiritual bodies. We invite you to clear all of your bodies daily and you will soon feel the difference between having a bright and clear aura or a field that is cluttered and dense.

Rest

Your body needs plenty of rest to function properly. Early to bed, early to rise is the recipe for a long life. In this way your body can truly replenish itself during the night. Many of you experience interrupted sleep due to the stressful living modern society so mercilessly demands. Heart disease, depression and hormone and organ dysfunction are only a few of the symptoms manifested by a body that can no longer restore itself in the way designed by nature. Your body has an in-built self-healing capacity, enabling it to deal with imbalances before they develop into serious illness. This magical self-healing system can only work when you treat your body appropriately.

In the future, the better known forms of eastern practices such as chi gong, tai chi, yoga and others, which raise the life force (chi or prana), will be taught as powerful tools of preventative medicine. Illness as you know it today will entirely disappear from the face of the earth. Most diseases stem from the ignorant treatment of your physical, emotional and mental bodies, and are completely avoidable. In the future the medical profession will use tools of prevention — cleansing, balancing and healing methods will be applied long before illness occurs in the physical body. Any form of sickness will be understood as a call from your soul, reminding you that you are out of balance and have overlooked certain aspects of life that need urgent correction.

In the New World, human beings will become more sensitive to their bodies and listen to the early signs of any imbalances. A skilled team of health professionals and healers will be able to assess the whole patient with their diagnosis, detect the true cause of illness and address it appropriately. This assessment will include factors such as life situation and circumstances, relationships, diet, exercise, rest, sleep patterns, internal as well as external causes of stress, emotional patterns and possible mental factors. They will also examine a person's spiritual alignment with their Higher Self and consider other diagnostic tools, currently unknown to humanity. Some holistic GPs, alternative health practitioners and skilled healers are already heading in this direction, addressing a variety of levels of consciousness as well as the outer circumstances contributing to the illness.

Stress release
The next important factor for your wellbeing is the release of negative emotions and stress that have been accumulated and stored in your physical body. If these energies get trapped and are not released regularly from your system, your body will become sick over time. This release can be achieved through yoga, chi gong, tai chi or other forms of physical activity, as well as massage, stretching, psychotherapy and breathwork. Unhealed emotions are often so intense and persistent that it is not sufficient to practise inner emotional healing to prevent their manifestation in your physical body. In these cases, physical forms of psychotherapy such as Bowen therapy, Core Energetics and others, as well as energetic massage, need to be applied to free your body from blockages.

Higher-self alignment
Premature ageing, which humanity has experienced for thousands of years, will become a distant memory. To arrive at this point, where longevity is no longer regarded as extraordinary, a deeper under-

standing of the immense impact of the alignment of your Higher Self on your physical form is necessary. Here lies the secret known to the true Masters since the beginning of time.

We would like to reveal a part of this secret. The light of Source is the most radiant and highest energy in the universe, the vibration of divine love and perfection. Where there is divine light, which is pure love and All That Is, there can be no sickness or ageing when you choose to be healthy and youthful. It is impossible. In the near future you will not see people ageing as you have throughout your lifetime. You will see 50-year-old people, and older, looking as agile and young as 35-year-olds. They will become living examples of the truth that we have revealed to you. In using the light of Source, you will no longer be tempted by surgical enhancements to provide you with a youthful appearance. This will, however, require your total surrender to the divine light and your full commitment to live according to the universal laws.

Life force
Another part of the secret of 'eternal youth' is the ancient knowledge of 'the science of life force'. These sacred energies emerge from the earth, flow through your meridian system and nurture you. Chinese medicine has been studying this science for over 5000 years. Tai chi and chi gong are techniques that demonstrate how to consciously access the healing powers of Mother Earth to provide you with a strong, healthy, youthful and agile body. The secret lies in combining, within you, these two powerful cosmic forces, the light of Source and the light of the earth, thus becoming the bridge between heaven and earth. Your four bodies influence each other, either in a positive or negative way, depending on your choices in life. Nothing is separate! Thoughts and emotions impact on your physical body, as does your state of consciousness, which is determined by the level of alignment to your spiritual body. A strong and healthy physical body will also

have a positive affect on the other three bodies. Walk in nature as often as you can. The invisible healing powers and the calming effects of Mother Nature are beyond your human imagination.

Super foods and vitamins
It is also worth commenting on super foods and supplements. The support that vitamins, minerals or super foods can provide is appropriate in times of recovery, rebuilding and stress. Yet they should not be seen as replacements for the above-mentioned positive attitudes and become a substitute for true responsibility. In this time of change, however, your bodies need more high-potency food to be able to deal with the ongoing transformation. You require less solid and heavy foods as your human bodies are becoming less dense. We recommend food high in nutrients such as green smoothies and other forms of liquid food.

Breath
Natural deep breathing is vital for your wellbeing as it allows the body to absorb the life force (prana, chi). Watch your breath and know that shallow breathing is a warning sign of your body being under stress. There are a number of breath work techniques available to release tension. In meditation, you can visualise inhaling white golden light, which is your true essence, and with each out breath releasing all negative thoughts, feelings and stress. Repeat this process until you feel a sense of calm.

The pace of life
To implement these changes, you will need to go against the trend of your modern times and slow down. Nothing of true value can be achieved if you continue to remain unconscious and run at an insane speed through your days. Nothing! You need to slow down.

In putting our suggestions into practice, you will soon discover that what humanity perceives as an entirely normal occurrence, such as the rapid ageing process and disease, is simply due to the incorrect use of the four bodies. The human body has been created in such a way that it can outlive the oldest person known on earth for decades, even hundreds of years. You will live in good health, without the need to age, when you finally discover who you truly are and learn to treat all bodies with the right knowledge and respect. Ageing, as it now occurs in the form of degeneration and wasting away, will be unknown in the future. Humanity is awakening and is taking a major leap in consciousness to become truly responsible. Learn how to live life. Do not be content with a shallow version of your true potential. Wake up! Only then can the New Golden Age come into manifestation.

32

ONENESS

We see the divine light in everyone and everything that exists, and we invite you to see through our eyes. In general, your perception of another person is nothing but your focus on their mask and shadow parts. This is also the way you often view yourself. From the viewpoint of absolute reality, this kind of perception is a total illusion. You identify yourself and others solely by the characteristics of limitation, learned behaviour, social conditioning and outer achievement, while we on the other side of the veil simply consider these as changing 'garments', worn by you during the journey throughout the ages. Your fears, hopes, pain and joy have created this mask and are perceived as your identity. From our side it seems almost unbelievable, but this way of perceiving has become your collective spell. Only in committing to inner healing and the spiritual path will you be able to break this spell and see what is real.

You are not what you believe you are. You are not a wife, a husband, a child, a doctor or a cleaning lady, someone needy, angry or frightened, someone intelligent or less educated. You are not a vegetarian or a McDonald's consumer, neither a Muslim nor a Christian, nor a Jew or Hindu. You are not what you are identifying with, whatever that might be. You are light and only light — light that has taken on many roles to experience life and lived through various levels of consciousness, even in other dimensions. You are born from Source, you are one with Source and with that you are one with everything, everyone and All That Is.

Dear ones, you set out long ago on this journey and began to believe that you are what you experience, forgetting that you are divine light — light that is immortal, almighty, beautiful, powerful, peaceful and eternal love: the Divine itself. Now is the time for you to remember your origin and return to where you once all came from. For this to happen you have to cease viewing yourself and your fellow humans as anything less than divine light. Your distorted perception of one another is based entirely on separation thinking and needs to be exchanged with the recognition of truth, acknowledging the light in yourself and others. Every time you think about someone, observe yourself and how you perceive this person. Do you see the light or rather their shortcomings and conditioned, limited behaviour? Do you perceive them as the roles they play, the job or title they hold? Are you willing to look behind their masks and see the eternal light — the true reality — and not get trapped in the living hologram you perceive as your world and falsely believe to be real?

Dear ones, your life on earth can be compared with the

'Holodeck' in the movie *Star Trek*, where people visit to have certain experiences. In *Star Trek*, however, the visitors to the Holodeck are aware of what they are doing and only go there to have an experience. They do not forget where they came from and who they are. This comparison with life on earth is more realistic than most of you would like to believe. You commit to the incarnation process with the full knowledge of who you are and where you are from, but after you pass through the veil of oblivion, most of you no longer remember your origin and get caught up in the game, entirely identifying with the role you have taken on to experience life from a certain angle.

You are all souls and are all equal. Although souls express differences in radiance and consciousness, you are all created by the One That Is. Only here on earth do you experience yourself as being separate from one another. This world was originally created with the intention to experience yourself as separate beings in a space of duality, but it was not intended that you would totally forget who you are. As time progressed, you accumulated more and more stories about yourself, perceptions about the world and each other. These stories became your reality, and as a result you were drawn back to earth again and again. You could also say you got stuck on the Holodeck and were unable to return to your star ship and fly home to where you belong. In terms of consciousness, this is exactly what has happened.

Now, at this crucial time in humanity's evolution, we are here to assist you in remembering where you once came from and who you truly are. Seeing the light in yourself and others will help you in this endeavour to see what is real. Begin to look behind the mask. Even a cruel mask is only a mask, and behind it lives the same shining light as within the one who wears a more pleasant mask. No mask is real, regardless of how real it might appear. Even though you perceive yourself as being separate and different from one another, there is only one divine light split into an infinite number of particles, which you meet in each other. This creates the illusion of the third dimension. This is the spell that needs to be broken.

We wish to open your eyes to the only reality that exists throughout time, space and all dimensions — the reality of Oneness of all beings, of all that exists. Your neighbour is the same light as you, even if he eats meat, while you are a vegetarian and is causing you trouble. Your mother is the same light as you, even if she has never meditated or done any inner healing. All of your apparent differences, your attempts to stand out from the masses, to be someone special, better than others or more spiritual, do not alter the fact that even a murderer carries the same light as a monk who helped the poor and meditated his whole life. You might question that a monk who has only done good and a murderer have the same light within. Nevertheless this is the truth. You may then ask whether it is worth doing anything to become more conscious, work on yourself and heal your wounds. Why start a journey requiring great effort, if a murderer has the same light as you? Well, you are the same light, yet the murderer wears a dense mask, preventing this beautiful light from fully expressing itself. Behind his cruel mask still lives the same light as within an enlightened teacher. The only difference is that the enlightened teacher has taken his mask off layer by layer, to allow more and more of his true light to shine through until there is no mask left — only divine light. The same light lives within both of them. This is where they are one, where you are all one with each other and where we are one with you.

We invite you to see with our eyes, the eyes of the Enlightened Ones. Our wish is for you to experience reality. See the light in each other rather than the shadow parts, which is an illusion anyway. You will see miracles occurring when you view the world through our eyes. Conflicts will disappear, understanding and constructive compromise will finally have an opportunity to bring peace, through seeing in each other that which unites. When this becomes your way of living, you will not only strengthen the light of others, you will also strengthen your own.

Every time you are ready to judge, to be aggressive and defensive, angry or hurt with respect to someone's actions, pause for a moment, take a deep breath and reflect on the underlying reason for these rising emotions. Remind yourself that it is the wounded part in your brother that is causing him to act in this harmful way. Why should you be upset with another person's behaviour when it was caused by his pain? Calmly put the appropriate boundary in place and remember who you truly are — you are divine light. Keep in mind that your fellow human is the same light as you and that you are one. You are one divine light, which is simultaneously having an infinite number of separate experiences of varying degrees of consciousness to expand itself.

You are part of this gigantic divine play; in actual fact you are the Divine. You are a cell in the great body of God, as is the one who caused you grief. So remember your Oneness with one another as often as you can. In doing so, you serve yourself and your brother. In living Oneness, which is the only reality, you assist Oneness to return to this world and for this world to return to Oneness.

33

RESPONSIBILITY

We would like to look deeper into a topic that most of you associate with uncomfortable feelings — responsibility. Can you sense your immediate reaction when you hear this word? Let us examine your understanding of it, for we believe it is your interpretation of responsibility that confuses you. In understanding its true meaning, you will no longer feel uncomfortable with this subject.

On the one hand, we observe some of you burdened by responsibility, while others are running away, fearing its chains. These contrasting reactions only express the extremes of the various misunderstandings surrounding this delicate matter. Let us share our view of true responsibility and compare our findings with what you generally believe responsibility to be. The difference will assist in shedding light on this issue. We consider your main responsibility as the one towards yourself — your own inner journey, how you walk through life — and the degree of integrity you put into practising what you believe to be true. This kind of responsibility is a big part of what human life is about. Ultimately, everyone is totally responsible for himself.

As an example, it is inappropriate to hold your parents solely responsible for your behaviour and shortcomings because their way of raising you was less than perfect. After all, following careful consideration, you were the one who chose them, including all of their shortcomings, as the ones to raise you and give you your first imprint for your journey on earth. It is often the shortcomings of your parents that bring forth your own wounds and limitations that you have carried from one life to the next. This is exactly why you chose this kind of environment: to bring your wounded parts to the surface in order that they may be healed. Without your parents 'pressing your buttons', your wounds would remain buried in your unconscious and you would be unable to recognise and cure them. In the end, you might even realise that your parents, with all of their imperfections, have done you a favour in unearthing your wounds.

We wish to encourage you to take full responsibility for all of your vulnerable aspects, caused by an imperfect childhood. Do not blame others; instead begin to see how things truly are. Learn to put appropriate boundaries in place and commit to your inner healing. Stop wasting your life energy on thoughts such as: 'If I could have had a better childhood, I would have achieved so much more in life.' Everyone experiences exactly the childhood he has chosen. It is about accepting what *is* if one is to truly break free. Dear ones, this is only one example of many where it is easy to escape into blame, but this is a waste of precious time and also missing the point. How often do you wish to hold someone else responsible for your feelings or life circumstances, someone such as your partner and children, friends, your boss and colleagues at work? In truth, no-one is responsible for your life except you. You are the only person who is responsible for your wellbeing, no-one else. This is your true responsibility. Not many of you know this simple truth and fewer live accordingly.

As we have previously mentioned, the focus of humanity is largely directed to the external world. There you all try to find answers that cannot be found, for your outside world is only a reflection of what lies within. Therefore, when you experience disrespect, put the necessary boundaries in place and look inside. Ask yourself: 'Do I truly respect myself and others?' You might be surprised by the answer, for it may reveal your disrespect for yourself or others. This negative behaviour could not affect you if the seed of disrespect did not first lie within. It is time for you to see what is real and how this world truly functions. Stop shadow-boxing and hunting phantoms by accusing and blaming others. If an unpleasant event occurs in your life, reflect on the true reasons for this situation. What has it to do with you? If you ask with perseverance and an open heart, you will receive an answer, providing you with another missing link in the puzzle called life. Do you realise that only through becoming fully responsible can this missing piece be given?

We have not only observed the avoidance of responsibility, but we have also seen some of you taking responsibility for others and mistaking this behaviour for love. We do not share this understanding with you, for everyone is responsible for himself. If you take responsibility for someone else in the belief that you are 'doing good', you are mistaken. It can also be said that you deny the other person the opportunity to learn and grow through doing the work themselves. In other words, you weaken them. So next time ask yourself if you are truly serving the other when you consider taking responsibility for them. We do not mean that you are not responsible for your children, pets, plants and handicapped or elderly people in your care. What we do say, however, is that your offer to help always needs to assist others to be as responsible as possible, for this is everyone's task on earth. Encourage those who need your care and love to be responsible. If you help in this way you are then aligned with your own and the other's soul purpose.

On the other hand, in taking the responsibility for another through misunderstood love, your behaviour is not in harmony with the Laws of Life and will serve neither you nor the other person. This kind of action will only create further weakness and dependency, which at some point in time you will both regret and resent. Besides the negative side effects for the receiver, this behaviour will also prevent the giver from accepting total responsibility for his own happiness, health and wellbeing. He will be unable to focus on his own healing work and inner journey, for he is too preoccupied with being responsible for others. As a result, neither the giver nor the receiver becomes responsible for himself. Interestingly, in the end the so-called 'good deed' served no-one.

When you assist someone, we ask that you do so with wisdom and discernment and encourage the one in need to be as responsible as possible. Only then will your support be of true help. You will both benefit greatly from this kind of wise assistance, for you are encouraging each other to grow more whole. This is true humanness — this is true love. Help one another to recognise the truth. You are not helping your fellow humans in supporting them to remain in their comfort zone, either purely out of habit or through feeling secure with the known. True love always aims to set the other free.

Your understanding of love is often the opposite, creating only further limitation and stagnation, which does not serve life. Always aim to serve life, true life, love, truth and inner peace with everything you do. With this attitude you cannot fail. The confusion existing on this planet regarding the true meaning of responsibility creates unnecessary but avoidable problems.

If you were to take full responsibility on a physical, emotional, mental and spiritual level, you would be more than occupied doing justice to this task. In doing so, you would feel less temptation to interfere with the business of others, which is theirs to resolve anyway. You would stop wasting your time controlling and manipulating others and develop a healthy attitude towards your fellow humans. You would gain insight into the truth that everyone creates their own life and only offer assistance when it is a stepping stone and true support for your brother to grow more responsible and loving. So much pain would simply disappear from this planet if you would truly understand responsibility.

We do not discourage you from helping one another; we do, however, ask that you learn to help with wisdom. Many of you who are in service to others forget to be truly responsible for your own wellbeing, which we consider to be an important human task on earth. Help others — 'Love your brother as you love yourself' — yet do not forget the second part of this commandment. Improve the lives of others by supporting them to become as responsible as possible for themselves on a physical, emotional, mental and spiritual level. It does not matter who it is. Your wife may want you to protect and defend her, regardless of whether she is right or wrong, your ageing parents might like to be carried on your shoulders or your children refuse to grow up. It might be your friends, who only demand your time to unload their burdens and lose themselves in pointless discussions, but never act upon your advice.

Become discerning. To learn how you can be of service to the world, talk less and observe more about yourself and your surroundings. Do not shy away from your true responsibility, which is to awaken to your divine self. At the same time, walk with an open, compassionate and loving heart through life. Lend your helping hand, with the wisdom of the sages, to encourage others to develop inner strength and take responsibility for themselves.

34

ATTACHMENT VERSUS DETACHMENT

Let us examine the true meaning of the terms attachment and detachment. Detachment is greatly feared by many spiritual students as a painful process and, because of this understanding, it becomes unnecessarily difficult. We would first like to have a closer look at the meaning of attachment, in order for you to comprehend why detachment is of vital importance if you truly wish to progress on the journey towards embodying your divine self.

So what is attachment? Attachment means false identification with, or falsely relating to, someone or something. Let us use an example to clarify this issue. If you are attached to someone in an unhealthy manner, this behaviour will dramatically limit your freedom to act, think and feel. If you are attached to the belief that you are what you own on a material level and the titles you hold, or you are identified with your youthful appearance and the beauty of your physical body, all of these beliefs will limit your consciousness instead of expanding it. If you 'love' someone so much that your focus is mainly on this beloved person, you misunderstand the true meaning of love. At the same time you will neglect your real task on earth, which is to establish a loving and supportive relationship with your human and divine self. These examples demonstrate that any form of attachment is a sign of being out of balance, preventing you from being who you truly are.

In the beginning of their lives all human beings need to form attachments in order to survive. Yet not always have you formed healthy attachments. These unhealthy forms of attachment are the subject we wish to discuss with you — the attachments that disconnect you from Source. When you decide to earnestly embark on your spiritual journey, there will come a time when you will be confronted with your attachments. This is the moment most of you fear. We beseech you, do not buy into fear. Fear only creates resistance, which again causes further unnecessary pain. When the time arrives to confront your attachments to the external world — situations you have greatly feared for lifetimes, unable to conquer until now — welcome them as your chance for learning. This simply means that you are ready and have created this opportunity on a higher plane to finally master this lesson and break free from your former limitations. In our eyes this is a moment of great joy and rejoicing.

Yet as long as you are still identified with your limited ego personality, you see things from a different perspective, and it will appear that you are going to lose what is dear to you. From the point of absolute reality, all of these scenarios look very different compared to the human perspective, where your view is always tainted by limitations of consciousness and your entanglement in the situation.

In actual fact, attachment derives from fear and means that you do not trust. You believe you have to hold on to something or someone in order to keep them, otherwise they would be taken from you. On the other hand, in a state of detachment you know that all is given and you do not need to hold onto anything or anyone, for that which serves you will always be with you and that which is no longer for your highest good will simply fall away.

If you accept the challenge to engage in the process of detachment and walk on your journey towards freedom, you will benefit greatly in asking your Higher Self for guidance. This will enable you to view your current life situation through the eyes of the Divine and you will receive valuable advice providing you with deep insights. With this new understanding, your steps will be lighter and more secure as you tread on the path into the unknown. Only there, where there is no trust, can the disciple of 'The Way' truly learn to trust. You cannot learn this important lesson when you have a safety net beneath you. You need to face your upcoming fears and overcome them step by step until you master the lesson. Never give your energy away to fear. This is the time of initiation, when it is required that you replace the mind with the heart. You will pass this challenging period faster and with the least suffering when you trust your heart, despite your mind constantly telling you that 'you must have gone insane'. This is the most confusing and threatening time for the human mind, which is used to having absolute rulership. Now it has to step aside and make space for the heart, open up to your soul and Higher Self and allow them to overtake the power.

Put yourself in the position of your mind and you can easily understand why it does not want to give up its control and will do its utmost to prevent this transformation from happening. Yet, if you want to make this process swift and as painless as possible, you have to surrender to your heart. The submission to your spiritual heart leads to reconnection with your divine self. No-one on the spiritual journey can bypass this crucial transition. Remember, there is great help at hand from the spiritual realms for the willing student of true life. However, you are the one who has to walk through your own darkness and fears.

After passing this initiation, you will realise what you feared most were nothing but phantoms made up lifetimes ago and nurtured through your fear. It is time to look through the illusion of fear and realise there is never anything to fear, only more to love, to make peace with and to forgive. Only naked can you walk through 'the eye of the needle' without false identifications and attachments keeping you small and limited. As you pass through to the other side, you will embody more of the light you are, and its wisdom, bliss and deep peace will envelop you.

In hindsight, many who have passed this test will ask themselves why they have feared this passage and resisted taking this step for so long. Now they have become aware that what they had to let go was small in comparison to what they have received, which is access to the greater self, where eternal love and peace reside beyond human comprehension. They might even admit that they would undertake the journey again, but this time without fear and resistance. They would walk in willingness, surrender and trust — into the arms of the Divine. This is called learning through insight, rather than suffering. We wish for all of you to choose this path of inner growth, for it is joyful and so much faster. Pain, created by resistance and holding on, is still a masterful but very uncomfortable teacher. It is about you making the conscious choice of truly walking your path, without halfway through again becoming victim to the temptations of the mind.

We do not judge you, no matter how you walk your journey. There are only less painful ways to master certain unavoidable passages of your inner path. You need to jump from the cliff and trust that your wings will grow as you fly. If you are able to walk on the edge of the razor blade and know deep inside that nothing can happen to you, you have truly gained freedom from your fear-based beliefs. You are home in the unlimited eternity, which is the only reality that exists. You will continue to live in the world, but no longer be of this world. Your spiritual heart is installed again and fully activated as your perfect connection device to the Divine. Then you will know that you are one with Source — *You Are Source.*

Step by step, your power and your divine knowledge will be given back to you. You walk as man, but with God's heart here on earth, to feed all who are thirsty for truth, peace and love. You will realise that what you once perceived as a dreadful event, before you passed the passage of detachment, in the end became a blessing. You will gain the understanding that nothing of true value was taken away from you, only your false beliefs and limitations. Yet what you have gained is of immeasurable value and can never, under any circumstances, be taken from you. You now know who you truly are, that you are one with God and that you are love. May our words inspire you to take a different, less reluctant, approach to the necessary transformation on your inner path — called detachment. This attitude will diminish your suffering and increase your insight into the necessity of this sacred process.

We want you to be excited about what awaits you when you pass through the portal of your heart. You will realise that what you have lost were only marbles and what you have gained are the most exquisite and purest of diamonds. We are waiting on the other side of the veil to welcome you home and share the joy with you, when you realise you are free — and free you have always been!

35

FREE WILL

Dear ones, let us examine the interesting topic of 'free will' — the true meaning behind this term and why we hold your 'free will' in such high regard. You may have heard that human beings are given free will by their Creator, which is indeed true. Yet few understand the importance of this gift and the full consequences of this divine bequest. Let us enlighten you. The gift of free will, bestowed upon every human soul, initially means that you have choice. The choice to do what you want — what feels right for you — to walk through God's creation as you please. You see, this is truly a gift, the total freedom to do whatever you wish. Yet, this gift comes with great responsibility, for you are accountable for your actions, thoughts and emotions. You are responsible for your deeds and all resulting consequences.

At this point, as we remind you of your responsibilities and the consequences of your actions, you might not be so sure that this is a gift you wish to accept. Well, this divine present has already been given to you as an immortal soul, and all who are here on planet earth have accepted it with the full awareness of its consequences and responsibilities, otherwise you would not be in this cycle of reincarnation.

We, who speak from the Heart of Creation, want you to understand why you were blessed with the freedom of choice. We did not wish to create you as puppets on strings, directed by supreme will. Instead we wanted you to be free to make the connection to your Origin, your Creator, out of longing for your true essence. The only way for this to happen was to grant you free will. What sense would it make if you were directed by a higher power and behaved like obedient robots, without having developed the ability to find out for yourself what is good, what is evil and everything in between? In order for all of you to develop the ability to make choices in alignment with your inherent light, we needed to let you walk free. Only through this gift of total freedom could we guarantee that your return to Source would be your choice, as would the time frame for this journey. This might seem a long and arduous process if you contemplate it from your perspective, limited by time and space. Yet it is quite a different scenario from our point of consciousness, where neither time nor space exists and all events are happening simultaneously. It is impossible to put our perception of this seemingly eternal process into human words, for we live in the eternal Now, where there is only love and no human judgment interfering.

Dear ones, here we touch on another important issue. As we have already mentioned several times during our teachings, we are without judgment. There is no judgment in this vast creation, only you as human beings appear to be preoccupied with this unhealthy concern, making your life and the life of others unnecessarily difficult. If freedom of choice is given to you and even the angelic and divine beings respect your decisions, why do you find the choices of your fellow man so hard to accept? Why won't you allow your brothers and sisters to find their own way? Souls express many different levels of consciousness and have their own way of learning on earth. Some of you might be advanced and experienced souls and your task is obviously different from the lessons a younger soul might look for.

Just because you are all in a human body does not mean that you are all here for the same learning. Would you judge a little baby for not participating in the final exams for a degree in maths at university? This is how absurd your judgment of others appears to us. We can clearly see 'who' is in a human body and why, which few of you are able to do. Most of the time your judgment is harsh and often the measures you take are completely inappropriate from our viewpoint of absolute reality. Simply because someone has come into old age does not mean this is a wise soul; it only indicates how many years someone has inhabited his human body. On the other hand, when someone lives in the physical body of a child, it does not necessarily mean this being is immature — it can sometimes be quite the opposite. We would like you to see with the eyes of your heart, which is the only way to perceive what is real. Have you not all at some point in time experienced wisdom coming from the lips of a child and nonsense from the mouth of an old man? Only when you learn to listen to your heart will you begin to understand.

On earth there are many different beings incarnated in human form. From the outside they all may appear the same, varying only at the level of age, gender and race. From the viewpoint of truth, their differences could not be any greater. They all come here for the same reason: to experience certain aspects of themselves through life on earth, which, in simple terms means to learn. Yet what they wish to learn differs greatly. Some might want to know what it feels like to be a victim, others to overcome victim consciousness. Some want to become leaders and train in certain aspects of true leadership, whereas others incarnate to experience power with all of its pitfalls and challenges. Some were born to learn about love and surrender and others came to wake up to their true nature. The reasons for incarnating are as different as all of you are, so why do you judge?

It might be that this soul you are condemning is experiencing exactly what it intended before it came into this world. We never judge, even when you get stuck in the same old pattern for lifetimes. In our eyes there is no reason for judgment, just opportunities for encouragement, support and giving advice on how to approach things differently next time. That does not mean you are not responsible for what you do — you indeed are! Your actions will determine the direction in which your future heads.

In the higher worlds punishment does not exist. This is an invention of your world, which is out of alignment with the Divine, and we cannot see the benefits of such actions. You cannot correct the so-called 'bad deeds' with negative actions, such as the various forms of punishment you use in your criminal correction facilities. Your high rate of re-offending speaks for itself. This loveless and ignorant treatment will soon disappear from the planet.

In the higher worlds, we have a well-trained team of guides and teachers who connect with a soul who failed to accomplish what it wanted to achieve in its human life. Together, they will examine the true reasons behind these failings and how the situation could be approached differently when experienced again. Most of the time this kind of support is sufficient to correct past mistakes, but not always. For the truly reluctant souls, we have places where they can stay in seclusion and relive again what they have done to others, until they are ready to master certain incomplete inner aspects. While we do not strive for perfection, we do strive for greater harmony and integration within every soul, which will one day reflect in the human being.

Dear ones, we wanted to show you how failure is handled in the higher worlds to inspire you to act in the same way. Stop judging yourselves, for judgment only holds you back from your own healing. Stop judging others, because you do not know why they are here on earth and act the way they do. Remember, some are still toddlers in terms of consciousness, just learning to walk. You would not judge a small child simply because you cannot discuss the latest politics or any other subject of your interest with him. Would you not like to help him to walk? Perhaps in the future you will support others to achieve what they are capable of and no longer try to force on them what is unsuitable according to their level of consciousness. Only the eyes of the heart can see. Train these eyes and use them as often as you can.

Look beyond your fragmented human perception if you wish to know what is real. Do not judge. Everyone has to carry the consequences of their actions and every action that is out of alignment with love and truth has to be balanced. This is the Law of Karma. If God is not judging you, why are you judging yourself and others so harshly? Perhaps you feel inspired by how we deal with failures and mistakes in the higher worlds and wish to apply this approach on earth. Your world would benefit greatly. There is only kindness and love, along with a firm assessment after the transition you call death, to support each being to a positive change, even for the ones you consider evil. Why should there not at least be more kindness, tolerance, acceptance and understanding for the choices your brothers and sisters make here on earth in free will?

36

DEATH

Let us lend you our eyes to examine the subject most feared by humanity. This fear is born from ignorance and is the reason for great pain and misunderstanding. Dear ones, today we wish to talk about the event you have named death.

You have all been born many times and died many times, so on a soul level you are familiar with the process of birth, which is the moment of entering your incarnation, and the transformation you call death, where you leave your physical body and exit your incarnation. Since most of you have no conscious memory of past lives, or of the life in between lives, you have to rely on the information provided by your cultural conditioning and religious upbringing. Regrettably, this second-hand knowledge determines your understanding of death. In the end you have no real knowledge, only inherited speculations, concerning the reality of death. As a result of this ignorance, the vast majority deeply fear death and avoid any acknowledgment of the fact that death is certain for every one of you. No-one who is alive on earth will escape death. Your fear of death is understandable but unhelpful, and giving in to this emotion makes little sense. If you fear something that much, as most of you fear death, why do you not want to learn as much as possible about this sacred transition? Why do you not wish to prepare for your death, to enable you to pass through this transition without fear?

For many thousands of years, sacred scripts have been written within all cultures about the mystery of death, which resemble each other in content. These holy texts speak of the process of dying as well as the journey the soul takes after leaving its physical form. Today few are familiar with these sacred books, and it is this ignorance of the true meaning of death that is creating deep-seated inner fear, turmoil and horror, passed on from one generation to the next. We believe it is time for humanity to be better informed and so break the chain of the heritage of fear once and for all.

At a certain point in time, you will all be confronted with your own death. Would it not be desirable to walk through this portal well prepared, fearless and knowing? In the not-too-distant future this is exactly what we see will come true. On the New Earth, death will lose its terror and human beings will be taught by wise teachers the true meaning of life and death. As it is an art to consciously birth a baby into the world, where the parents prepare themselves with courses, exercises and literature for this joyful event, the same care and attention applies for your passage into the other world when you know your time to leave has come. Despite the obvious fact that none of you can escape death, most of you avoid any thought of it and, when the time for passing over arrives, it is perceived that 'great tragedy has struck'. Nothing 'strikes you' by chance. As we have previously mentioned, you all plan on a soul level the exact time of your birth as you do your leaving.

You need to leave your limited and false beliefs about death behind and heal your fears. Your bookstores are filled with research about this very subject — ancient books of death, reports of near-death experiences and more. Some books will enlighten you; others may not. It is about you using discernment to find what rings true in your heart. Never before since the fall of Atlantis has so much valuable and true information about death and dying been so freely available for everyone on this planet. You need to understand that what most of you believe in general about death is a mass deception and it is truly time for humanity to break this spell. Death is a sacred transition, not so different from birth, simply the other way around. At birth, you open the portal to enter this world, and in death you use the same portal to leave the earth to return to where you came from. You will again recognise yourself as the immortal soul you are, as you did before you took on a body of flesh.

Why should the process of leaving be accompanied by such agony, fear, pain and desperation, when your arrival is so joyfully celebrated? Your fear is connected to the flawed belief that life ends with the death of your physical body, which of course is not true. In fact, you all exist in the spirit world before you are born — a world that is just as real as the experience of earthly life. You need to understand that this incarnation is not your whole life. It is only a short experience in the vastness of your life as an immortal soul. If you recognise your own immortality, your outlook on death will change significantly and the death of your physical form will be less traumatic, which will be healing and freeing. This does not mean that there will be no grieving when a loved one passes over, but the grief will be lessened and your recovery swifter, no longer life-crippling as it is today.

So let us share with you what truly happens at this sacred

transition. When your experience on earth is coming to an end, you will leave this body with its particular personality behind, to again unite with the vast consciousness of your immortal soul. You will be reunited with your soul family on the other side of the veil in great joy. You will celebrate together if you have completed what you intended to accomplish in your earth life. There is no reason to give up living and be inconsolable for a long period of time because one of your loved ones has passed over. We understand that a certain amount of grief is healthy and necessary; yet most grief derives from the stern belief in the illusion that death is 'the end' and your beloved has ceased to exist. Every one of you, without exception, survives death and has done so many times before. Your death in this life is not your first, and for the majority of you will not be your last.

So why not closely examine that which you fear most? At the moment of death your immortal soul, providing you with life force and attached to your physical body through the silver cord, becomes disconnected through the cutting of this cord and leaves. In the hours and days after death, the etheric, emotional and mental bodies slowly dissolve and in this process, your soul distances itself from the personality it has taken on through the physical body. This means it leaves its human limitations and identifications behind and opens up to the vastness of its own divine light. On the other side, the soul is met by guides, soul companions and loved ones to welcome it home. It is a time of great joy and reunion, not only with the greater consciousness of your own essence, but also with other souls with whom you have built strong bonds.

Remember, in this environment there is no time, and events that would last many days on earth can be experienced within a few minutes. After the joy of the reunion, the moment arrives when you will assess your last incarnation with the help of a guide or alone, whatever is more suitable for you. Dear ones, there is no-one judging you for what you have or have not done in your earthly life — no-one besides you. You are your own strictest critic, not your guides or teachers. The love and compassion existing on the other side of the veil are incomprehensible and almost unimaginable for you, who are used to widespread judgment on earth. The world of your soul and life on earth have little in common with one another, at least on this level, where a thorough assessment of your human existence will be undertaken in the space of unconditional love, understanding and encouragement. You will review your life and then be encouraged to look at situations where you could have used more courage, love or wisdom, but always without judgment. Judgment is a human attitude and has no place in the worlds of higher vibration.

You will then meet 'the Council of Elders', where you will be lovingly supported in assessing the life just passed and evaluating what you intended to learn, as well as in considering different possibilities to strengthen your remaining weaknesses. You will receive advice on how to balance your energies more efficiently to enable you to reach your set goal. At these meetings, you will experience a rapid karmic review, spanning centuries, to provide you with greater insights into your inner path.

Some souls might consider reincarnation fairly quickly, while others decide on a break and remain in the spirit world for a longer period. No-one is forced to reincarnate; everyone has first to understand the consequences and lessons of his previous life. If, for example, you have hurt others, you will relive the same situation in the position of the other person, to better comprehend the impact of your thoughtless actions. This experience is not meant as punishment; it only serves the purpose of better understanding and learning. If you are reluctant to learn certain lessons, you will not be forced, for in the spirit world guides and teachers always accept 'the Law of Free Will'. Yet you cannot move on or participate in certain activities of higher learning until you have mastered your lessons.

There is so much more to share about life after death that could easily fill volumes, but for now we do not intend to go into greater detail. We simply wish to open your limited perception of the transformation called death and ease unnecessary fears.

There is, however, another important event we would like to mention, which will take place immediately after you leave your physical form. It is described by those who have had a near-death experience as going into a bright, white light of pure love and unspeakable bliss. This is your own Higher Self Presence over lighting your soul while you are passing over. This light is also a part of The Presence — Source — The Creator. No human words are able to describe the bliss, peace and love you will experience as you enter the divine light. You will feel the deep longing to remain there forever. Yet, in order to stay in union with the Divine Presence for all times, a soul has to continue to strive towards Oneness with the Divine, which is All That Is. When there are only love, peace and truth left within you, and nothing but this every single moment, you will know you are home and remain in the presence of The Presence eternally. We are speaking from this consciousness, for All That Is is what we are.

You need to understand that your soul is immortal and your life is eternal. You all pass through various experiences, whether in physical incarnation or without physical form. Alternatively, you could also say that you only have one life, which is your eternal life, spent in many different bodies and in varying stages of consciousness. If you comprehend this truth, you will completely lose the fear of death.

We hope that we have enlightened you about the painful and frightening topic you have given the name death. Our wish is to see you becoming more interested in studying the process of death, dying and the afterlife. As we have previously mentioned, your bookstores are filled with information about this subject. Let your heart guide you to the right teachings. We bless you, as you are all on the path walking towards your divine light.

37

FIGHT

As long as human beings believe in fight, they will remain caught in duality. Duality is an illusion, preventing you from seeing reality as it truly is. Reality can solely be perceived from the consciousness of Oneness with All That Is. Some of you are convinced that, when you have taken your first steps towards the light, you need to fight that which you perceive as darkness. This is a fundamental error of perception and stems from limited fear-based beliefs.

Imagine there is a dark room and then you switch on the light. Did the light fight the darkness in the room? Certainly not. The light simply enlightened the darkness, which is an entirely different process to fighting the darkness. If you fight the darkness, your focus is on what you do not want, the darkness. In actual fact, you strengthen what you oppose by directing your energetic focus to it. Instead of wasting your precious life with this pointless endeavour, it is better to give your attention to the light. To enlighten a room, focus on the light. Wherever you direct your attention, there too is your energy, and manifestation follows energy. Focus your energy on what you want to see in your life and in this world.

Dear ones, we wish to teach you how to end the fight and act from wisdom. In not wasting your energy in fight, by not using force, the light enlightens the darkness and in this way its true power becomes visible. Do you know the difference between force and power? Force tries to manipulate, control and convince, whereas true power acts out of the certainty of its own innermost essence, which is truth, peace and love — it just *is*. Force is weak, for it is uncertain of itself and needs to fight against someone or something to prove itself. Power simply knows and *is*. What a difference. Force moves fast, is suspicious, manipulative and controlling. True power is none of these. Power is still, so still that there is no movement, not even a word needs to be said. Power radiates its light to everyone and everything by simply being.

Take the image of a pebble dropping into a lake. Imagine the rings emerging from the centre where the pebble fell into the water. One circle after another appears effortlessly from within. This is how true power works: it radiates from the essence of its being in total stillness and its reach is far. Envisage a child refusing your guidance and advice and, despite all of your well-meaning explanations, it stubbornly insists on its own will. If you go into confrontation and begin a fight with this little guy, you will only strengthen his resistance and persistence or force him into submission. Yet, if you lovingly redirect his attention towards your goal with positive encouragement, you will quickly reach your desired aim, without losing yourself in an unnecessary battle of wills. These small examples demonstrate how pointless fight is and why we ask that you cease the fight.

Fight is a deeply ingrained habit on this planet. Dear friends, as we have previously mentioned, it is time for you to grow up. You need to realise that you have passed the stage where ignorant and destructive behaviour is tolerable. Unfortunately, most human beings still live in fight, an inner fight with themselves as well as being involved in various outer fights with partners, friends, parents or work colleagues. Nation against nation, religion against religion, company against company, woman against woman, man against man, men against women, spiritual people against atheists, one political party against another, one race against the other and so on. We believe we have named enough examples to demonstrate that fight is one of the most common daily occupations on earth. We are aware that you are not used to viewing things the way we perceive them; nevertheless, we see the need to speak the truth. What we categorise as fight, you might call 'healthy competition', yet at its core this act is nothing but fight — one against the other. Where is the respect for the free will of your fellow humans? Where is your compassion — your love? There is no inner peace within you. For most of your waking hours, you are preoccupied with manipulating and convincing others to act your way. Despite well-meaning intentions, the majority of you are unaware of the fact that you are acting violently towards one another and at times using 'emotional and mental war techniques' to achieve your goal. This kind of behaviour can be observed in most conflicts in partnerships and also in spiritual discourses, where one student wants to convince the other that 'the truth' he has found is more profound than the one of his fellow human. You can also notice the same attitudes in heated discussions in companies, your political landscape, in other institutions, as well as in families, where everyone is required to align to a certain code of conduct and no-one is truly allowed to be himself.

Dear ones, we want you to understand that if you wish to have a better world or desire a family that stands together, you need to live what you believe in. You cannot force your ideas on others. Every one of you can only learn through true insight — when the soul is ready. If you act from truth and inner peace, give space to one another and respect the choices of others — the seeds you sow with your integral behaviour will blossom in their own time. Yet, even with the best of intentions, if you try to force your insights upon others, these seeds will fall on barren ground, dry up and die. If you talk about love and peace, you have to be love and peace. You cannot preach love, but you are all able to feel love and peace truly radiating from the heart. This kind of experience will create openness in your fellow man, which forceful words would never achieve. If you want to see change — whether personally, in your career or in any other environment — you have to *be* the change you want to see in this world. Do not get stuck in complaining about the apparent lack of love leading you to despise the world or others. Instead, *be* the love you seek and the peace you are longing for. True power performs miracles, as it radiates from the core of your innermost essence and manifests through your words and actions.

We trust we have enlightened you about the power of love and peace and clearly pointed out the failings of the force of fight. So lay your weapons down. Understand, we are all one and we mean everyone is one with everyone. Act from the true centre of your being, which is Love. Learn step by step to use the power anchored in the wisdom and peace of your heart.

It is not always necessary that both opponents involved in a fight make the shift to peace and love in acknowledging their Oneness, even though this would be preferable. Usually it is sufficient when one transforms his destructive behaviour. This will energetically turn the whole situation around and help to resolve the conflict. The energy you put into a fight — even if it is a fight for a good cause — will always further feed fight. On the other hand, when you direct your focus towards respect, understanding and tolerance for the other's choices, by peacefully holding your attention on the goal, you will feel a sudden shift in the whole scenario. You will then observe the resistance of your opponent lessening, simply because your energy is no longer directed against him. Instead, it is focused on your goal in a peaceful manner and the other can sense your openness. This is the moment when your brother has for the first time the opportunity to truly hear you. Before, he was primarily occupied with his defence or attack. Since this is no longer necessary, he is able to open up, which was impossible under the condition of fight. The fastest way to create understanding and true peace is for you to *become* peace.

Let us consider another interesting aspect, when you are confronted with a situation where you have to choose between force and power. Force is always born from fear. This could be the fear that you feel when you are not heard and seen for who you really are and as a result are unable to present your point of view. This means that whenever you are acting from an unhealed inner space, you are not centred nor are you aware of what you are doing. True power, on the other hand, derives from deep inner knowing and simply acts from the wisdom of your innermost being.

This is the significant difference between a warrior and a peaceful warrior. A warrior still remains victim to his own insecurities and is driven by negative emotions such as anger and rage. Even the noble fight for justice can trigger him to fight with force. Consequently, his actions come from a point of weakness, regardless of how strong his physical appearance and words might appear, as his underlying motivations remain driven by his unhealed wounds. On the contrary, a peaceful warrior has found peace within himself. He lives in alignment with his soul and Higher Self, never attacks but simply uses the energy of his aggressor to redirect it towards a better solution, or if necessary his own defence. This is the only kind of action that will bring about peace, whereas the deeds of the unhealed warrior always lead to greater conflict.

It is easy to understand the reason for this outcome when you examine the motivation behind these forceful actions, which are created by fear. The result of all fear-based actions will always be the same, namely to create further fear. Every action birthed from fear will lead to greater fear. Yet all you do from the space of love, peace, understanding and respect will result in valuable insights, greater love and deeper peace. Beloveds, learn discernment, observe yourself and be aware of where your actions come from. Do they come from fear or love? There is never anything in between. When they spring from fear, heal this fear and replace it with love. Let love become your main intention and motivation for everything you do. The fear, seducing you to choose force over power, always stems from the wounded child inside.

It is time for humanity to collectively heal their inner child. Only then can the wounded child turn into the 'wonder child' who holds the keys to heaven, leading you to the union with your True Self. Remember, unless you adopt the path of total harmlessness towards all sentient beings, including yourself, you will remain unable to experience lasting peace on earth.

We began this chapter with the word 'fight' and ended with love. As it is with all stories, when the last story ends it ends with love. You all come from love, lose yourself in fear and inner and outer fight, and finally return to love. May peace and love be with you and guide you home.

38

SPIRITUAL BYPASSING

We wish to examine this important subject of using spiritual and religious practises to a cover up unpleasant and difficult emotions. These practices have not been given to mask or escape your pain of the past. When we use the term past, we not only mean your upbringing in this life, we also include all experiences from previous lifetimes. Everyone of you is filled with memories of pain and fear, leading to the creation of a mask. The purpose of this mask is to guarantee your survival and prevent further suffering — this is at least the subconscious intention and the reason why your mask was created. Yet the mask's protection is only temporary and superficial, and in the end it prevents you from expressing your true nature. Real protection against recurring pain is only possible when you face your fears and heal your pain. Yet our observation is that many traditional spiritual and religious teachings do not sufficiently address the healing of the emotional aspect. As a result, these teachings are in this regard outdated or, to say the least, incomplete.

Until a hundred years ago, human beings with a few exceptions had no understanding of the impact of their emotions. Nevertheless, everyone was still ruled by them, as it is the case today, but no-one knew how to address the pain. This attitude changed significantly when Sigmund Freud published his findings, which later inspired countless fellow researchers, to investigate the unknown field of the human psyche and develop further theories of healing. We regard the birth of psychology as a momentous turning point in human history. Yet it must be acknowledged that it took almost 100 years for the main principles of these findings to reach the mainstream and influence mass consciousness. In contemplating this fact, it becomes clear that all previous religious and spiritual teachings were untouched by these essential findings, for the time of their foundation was centuries or even thousands of years earlier.

We want to invite you to work with spiritual practises in conjunction with psychological healing techniques, in order to develop a more integrated approach on your journey towards wholeness. As previously mentioned, almost all spiritual teachings were significantly altered through established religions ignoring self-love as one of the most fundamental foundations of the inner path. Through this neglect and denial, spiritual teachings turned into an all too exclusive pathway for a chosen few instead of offering salvation to every soul, as it was their intended purpose.

In fact, most religious and spiritual teachings were therefore only covering up and silencing the pain within. You were told to be obedient to your spiritual or religious rules and expected to live by their virtues. Yet as long as your underlaying fears and pain remained unhealed, all behavioural changes could only be superficial and little more than make-up, layered upon your wounds, instead of developing healthy spiritual attitudes flowing naturally from your innermost essence. In not healing your pain in the first place, and then trying to force yourself to live in accordance with these virtues, many spiritual and religious teachings have reversed steps 1 and 2. So it comes as no surprise that despite all well-meaning attempts, the majority of you still feel unable to achieve lasting inner change.

Fear and feelings of unworthiness underpin almost all human actions and behaviour. Yet the good news is that for the first time in your known history, there is a vast selection of healing methods available for everyone.

You need to understand that you cannot act according to your virtues and live in spiritual alignment as long as there is anger, sadness, fear and other negative emotions smouldering like a slow burning fire within. In general your response towards these unwanted emotions is suppression and as a result, your emotions become frozen and end up being stored in your physical body. This is unfortunate, because stored emotions are a major contributing factor to all physical and mental illness. Yet this is how the majority of you deal with negative emotions — by either silencing them or dwelling on them. Both of these choices are unhealthy and destructive, blocking the flow of your life force.

Furthermore, this behaviour also leads to serious imbalances and a misalignment with your soul and Higher Self. It is time to find a new and more constructive approach in dealing with painful and unwanted emotions. The simplest way is to compassionately listen to these parts of you, crying out for love and attention.

In your childhood, most of you were seldom seen for who you truly are. Nearly all human beings carry these aspects of the wounded child within. If these parts are left untreated, they will affect all of your actions and reactions towards your surroundings and the way you treat yourself. The majority of human beings are literally directed by their wounds and at the same time completely oblivious to the dire consequences of this behaviour. For your better understanding, we would like to give you a few examples of what it means to be influenced by the wounded inner child. For instance, if you feel the need to be controlling and manipulative or if the success in your job is driven by the inner craving to be finally good enough and to be loved, the wounded child is ruling you. It also has you under its control when you choose force over true power or remain stuck in victim consciousness, jealousy or you feel unable to forgive. You can also be assured that your wounded inner child is in charge when you are convinced that you have to work hard to be loved. The same applies for all feelings of unworthiness.

We believe that all of you are familiar with these painful emotions. There are countless ways to cover up negative emotions. You only have to look at the range of addictions exactly serving this purpose, such as all types of drug and alcohol abuse, sex and food addiction, work and shopping addiction, obsessive-compulsive disorders and other mental illnesses. When it comes to covering up and suppressing pain, there are plenty of choices. The only result of this unfortunate behaviour is that your unwanted emotions remain trapped in your body until they are triggered, and then the whole cycle repeats itself. Many of you recognise that this cannot be the solution, and more people than ever before are reaching out for help and turning to different forms of healing and therapy.

We would also like to mention another form of suppression of negative emotions by using spiritual practises for example meditation as a way of avoiding pain by bypassing the emotion and escaping into the spiritual realms. This behaviour can only lead you to being severely ungrounded and to lose yourself in illusions on a spiritual level.

The ability to become 'the observer', means to be able to watch yourself in a non judgemental, neutral manner when faced with a difficult situation or inner conflict, removed from the identification of the emotional turmoil of your wounded aspects. This is a crucial and beneficial therapeutic technique that can shorten your healing process and lead you safely through the challenging times of inner transformation. When you do not develop the ability to observe yourself, the danger arises that you will completely identify with these strong emotions, allowing them to twist your reality. You may even believe that this is truly 'you' experiencing these feelings, whereas in truth it is only a small unhealed aspect of your whole self expressing its fears and pain. The process of healing can therefore become long and confusing if this simple but valuable method is not applied.

We would like to provide you with another example of healing. When you acknowledge the unexpressed anger you felt as a child, you will be able to follow your spiritual teachings, asking you to no longer act from a space of anger. You will release this anger and learn to put proper boundaries into place, allowing you to deal with others who are unable to see you for who you are, in a healthier and more constructive manner. You will discover your self-worth and finally acknowledge yourself, for you will now comprehend that you will first need to give love, respect, attention and acknowledgment to yourself, instead of desperately longing to receive it from others. No guru, therapist, psychologist, priest or spiritual teacher can do this work for you. It is *your* wounded inner part. Only *you* can heal this broken aspect within. In healing yourself, you will be able to reach your spiritual goals with unknown ease.

Until today, many of you tried to force themselves to live by spiritual rules and virtues. We would rather see you letting go of all use of force and instead become more loving towards your human aspects and your fellow man. Our wish is for you to *be* love. Love is 'the Reason for all Being', 'the Cause of Creation' and the core of all that you name spiritual. Yet all too many seekers try to reach their spiritual goals with vehement force directed against themselves. Spiritual self-flagellation is just one extreme example of an external physical act that visibly demonstrates what countless students of the spiritual path are doing to themselves on an inner level. It is time to end this nonsense, for it is only causing harm and does not lead you to true liberation. There is no other way than to love yourself with all of your imperfections and then heal them layer by layer. You need to love yourself home. In following the 'Path of Love', your spiritual transformation will become a joyful process. Step by step, you will overcome your destructive behaviour and heal your negative emotions. As a result of this cure, your actions will naturally align with your chosen spiritual discipline.

You will experience deep inner peace and contentment when living in alignment with love. You could compare your self-destructive behaviour with the following analogy. Imagine you have a hungry, sick horse and, despite its weakness, you continue to beat the poor creature because it does not perform like a prized racehorse. Would it not be wiser and more compassionate to first feed, heal and care for this being, so that at a later point in time it can be trained and may even have the chance to participate in a race?

We believe that we have made our point clear concerning the urgency of your inner healing. This is the foundation from which true spiritual discipline can grow, ensuring your path will be successful. The seriousness and rigidity that mark the spiritual journey of too many seekers simply demonstrates that they have not yet understood this lesson. We invite you to take the time to listen to your tears, cries and anger in the most loving and non-judgmental manner. In doing so, your suffering will lessen and the journey to spiritual mastership can truly begin. Remember you do not have to be someone special. Be yourself: this is enough for your Creator, should it not be enough for you? Relax and watch the miracle of the power of love transforming weakness into strength and your tears into the jewels of your crystal crown.

We wish to add some further remarks concerning the interest and the popularity of the teachings of 'the Law of Attraction'. When these techniques are practised without emotional healing and proper spiritual alignment to the higher self, they can only lead to the senseless and pointless fulfilment of ego desires, which is not the original purpose of this divine law.

39

YOU CHOOSE THE CIRCUMSTANCES OF YOUR LIFE

Let us investigate an interesting topic: the choices your soul makes prior to incarnating on earth. As we have previously mentioned, all of you chose your parents and also made agreements to meet other souls at certain points in time on your journey through life. These souls will play a significant role in helping you to achieve your set goals in this incarnation. Some souls will support you, while others will appear to act more in the role of an antagonist, causing pain and difficulties.

These souls could be considered your counterparts, as they challenge you and at times even try to pull you in the opposite direction from where you want to go, to test your inner strength and bring up hidden fears. You tend to have negative feelings towards these souls, who have agreed to play this part in your life and 'press your buttons'. Yet we consider this perception as lacking truth and wisdom, for it does not reflect the deep love you both feel for one another on the other side of the veil.

We will explain our viewpoint, which as you know by now is different from yours, as we are able to see you on both sides of the veil. On the one hand, we observe you fully involved in your present human life with its joy, challenges and limitations, and we also see all of your other incarnations simultaneously. Remember, time is an illusion and does not exist from where we speak. Only you on earth perceive events on a linear timeline, whereas from our perspective everything is Now — everything that ever happened since your creation and will ever happen is Now. We also see you as an immortal soul that made conscious choices for this incarnation while in the spiritual world. In addition, we know you as your eternal Higher Self, which is untouched by limitations and a part of Source, the aspect of you that never left home. You see, our perception of you differs greatly from what most of you perceive as your identity. You consider only the body and personality of your current incarnation as being 'you', whereas we regard this perception of yourself as being only a small part of your existence. Our image of you is far beyond the average human comprehension.

Let us focus on the time when you decide to incarnate on earth and choose your physical body, birth family and a variety of circumstances that will influence this life. Again, we need to state that no-one is forced to incarnate, nor are you forced into a particular embodiment, even when you believe at certain times that your life is too difficult and you blame God or destiny for the misery you are experiencing. Your choice has nothing to do with God. God gave you free will and this applies on both sides of the veil.

Let us turn our attention to a point before your incarnation where you review and discuss your next life with your teachers or guides. You carefully contemplate the advantages and disadvantages of every choice you have, in order to lead you to your desired goal. Let us assume you wish to learn about compassion and you receive the offer for your next life to become the parent of a handicapped child who needs your lifelong care and support. Or you are given the opportunity to live in the slums of a third world country, where you can learn great compassion through not getting caught up in your own misery; instead you can help to ease the suffering of your fellow humans. Can you see what we mean? On a soul level, you are only interested in the desired result and do not ponder having a life of convenience, which most of you desire when incarnated on earth.

Let us take another example: you meet someone in your twenties who you feel strongly attracted to and marry. Your partner does not treat you well and is unable to give you respect, appreciation, love, understanding and support. Unfortunately, you realise he has these disturbing attributes after the birth of your first child. From a human point of view, this relationship is a disaster, but from your soul's perspective it is the perfect match, for it brings to the surface your unhealed parts, which are mirrored by your partner's abusive behaviour. You continue to believe in your bad luck, until you realise that the other is only reflecting what you do to yourself. Your soul only sees that this marriage serves as an important catalyst to bring your unconscious self-sabotage to the surface, which is the first step to healing.

Here is another example: someone fights, blackmails and tells lies about you, which you consider a dreadful situation. Your soul, however, does not think this way, for it is aware of your whole story, where in a number of incarnations you had repeatedly faced these kinds of painful situations and, as a result of these experiences, you gave up the will to live. You lost your power and begged for justice, but nobody believed you and in the end you lost trust in yourself. Your soul has chosen to work on this particular emotional injury and sent you someone who repeats this dreaded scenario. This time, it is your opportunity to learn to stand in your power without giving your energy away to false accusations and rumours and in turn overcome the pain and limitations of many lifetimes.

Can you see the wisdom in this choice of your soul? Most of you, when incarnated, tend to wish for a comfortable and successful life, without tragedy and too many challenges, but what would you learn from it? Sometimes souls choose an uneventful life to rest for a short while, but this is rare, for rest and rejuvenation are normally experienced in the lifetime between lives. Generally, rest is not the purpose of coming to earth. Earth experience is desired by many souls for several reasons. Incarnations serve as an opportunity to learn and develop certain abilities, or to test your capacity to withstand the pull into oblivion and still be true to your inner values, regardless of how strong the polarity and density on this planet are affecting you.

You also come to earth for the enjoyment of being in a physical world. Souls generally exist in the astral, higher causal and spiritual worlds, where they are able to experience any form they like, except dense physicality such as on earth. Most importantly, the majority choose reincarnation to rebalance their karma, which in the end means to balance themselves from within. Eventually, even the most reluctant soul wants to learn and progress towards expressing their inner light. This is the natural thrust of evolution, which cannot be forced and is never forced upon you.

We believe you have gained important insights and now understand that your soul has chosen, after careful consideration, all aspects and circumstances of your life, for you to grow. If you are in a difficult and painful life situation, we invite you to go deep within. Learn to connect with your soul and Higher Self, to better understand your challenges and ask for divine guidance. Ask your soul to help you to understand what lies behind your life situation. It will serve you well to learn from your soul's wisdom and explanations. At all times help is there for those who ask. Learn to observe yourself and see conflicting events from a soul level and you will slowly gain a deeper understanding of these situations and people coming into your life. There is always a significant reason behind each of these experiences. If you have suffered betrayal in many lifetimes, it is not meant as punishment that you experience a simular scenario in this life. Your soul may have chosen this recurrence of events as the chance for you to finally forgive those who betrayed you. This situation may also benefit you in learning how to remain unaffected by the actions of others.

These are a few of countless examples that could be given to illustrate the wisdom hidden behind unpleasant or even tragic events. Do not waste your energy and precious time with complaints about your life. You made the choice. Every day it is up to you either to deal with what unfolds in your life or to refuse to take responsibility and continue to live as a frustrated victim of an apparent unfair destiny. If someone suffers, it can be that he has caused suffering to others in a previous life, but this is not always the case. The delicate balance of the law of karma works on a more refined level and can only be understood with the eyes of love and without judgment. Only through love will truth reveal itself to you.

Do not even try to figure out the underlying reasons why someone else has to go through difficult times. As long as you have not achieved union with your divine self through the total surrender of your heart, you can only rely on your mind, which is not equipped to comprehend the greater picture. We prefer that you look at yourself to understand what lies hidden behind these events in your life and meetings with others. We assure you this task will require your full attention. When you totally accept all experiences and adopt the wisdom of non-resistance, you will see life as an opportunity to grow. Furthermore, you will perceive your earthly life as a chance for healing, and your soul's intention for this incarnation will be revealed. In the end, you will have deep gratitude for everything you have experienced in your life, whether it is the pleasant encounters or the painful ones. You may even feel more grateful for the times of suffering, for they enabled you to outgrow your limitations, which was exactly the intended purpose of your soul for these events to unfold in this life.

40

Awakening and Enlightenment

When you have liberated yourself from all limited concepts and perceptions and completed your spiritual initiations, you will reach a state of consciousness where divine grace unfolds its sacred wings. You will realise that you are free — absolutely free. Joy will fill your whole being, as you look at yourself and recognise the effort with which you have lived life and walked your inner journey. In fact, you will become aware that it was this fierce effort, and your beliefs born from fear, which prevented you from fully acknowledging your divinity.

You now understand that you have always been free. Then, only one law remains — to be Love. You will feel deep joy within your heart celebrating your homecoming. You will also rejoice with your soul friends and teachers on the other side of the veil, for you are finally liberated from the chains of judgment, concepts and limitations. The whole universe sings with you, for you experience and perceive clearly the divine light you are and have always been. Glory in the heavens! Tremendous joy fills everyone who completes the journey home, while still bound to one's earthly body. You have pierced through the veil, leaving behind pain and suffering caused by the stern belief in fear and identification with your ego self. Legions of angels and enlightened beings will surround you as you reach this important step on your journey. On earth you call this state of consciousness 'awakening'. This is the first stage of enlightenment.

We would like to have a closer look at the inner development that follows your return from separation. Your human heart has made space for your divine heart and your divine heart is now guiding you every step of the way. Everything in you has surrendered to the sacred heart and acknowledged its greater wisdom. The human part in you has stepped back and made space for your immortal soul. Your soul then surrendered to your Higher Self, allowing the brilliance of the light of the Divine to overtake guidance.

This is the secret that alchemists have been looking for in the external world, with their attempts to transform lead into pure gold. The alchemistic principle of turning lead into gold is also a metaphor, describing the transformation of the human self and its soul into the divine self. Some who have reached this stage of divine union are able to create so-called miracles. Yet we wish to emphasise that it is not about the performance of a miracle in itself, for a miracle will only occur as a 'by-product' of enlightenment. That is to say, those who have mastered all aspects of themselves are given the power to master the elements, the substance from which everything in the universe is created. Unexplained physical healings may then occur, for your bodies are built from these elements. The elements will obey the higher divine order, as pure Source light is streaming through the healer, if healing is for the highest good of everyone involved, in tune with the laws of karma and supporting the goals this soul has set for himself in this particular incarnation.

An awakened soul represents only the 'kindergarten stage' of enlightenment and has to be considered as this. Some who attain this level of consciousness believe they have reached the final goal, which is an illusion. There is always more to learn on every level of consciousness. Even the teachers you call Masters or the Enlightened Ones, who have reached unimaginable levels of Oneness with the Divine, are forever refining and rebalancing themselves, and their learning is constant. So put this kind of thinking aside and know that you have reached a new level of consciousness, not unlike that of a newborn child, which needs to reorientate itself and study the lessons of this particular stage of consciousness. Humility, as a lived virtue, will always serve you well regardless of how advanced your present state of consciousness might appear to you. Be aware that there is always a level above where you will gain greater insights.

You can also say that one general law applies at all times. If you wish to move to the next level of consciousness, you have to be willing to let go of all that you believe you are and all of your learned knowledge. In order to expand your light, you have to pass through 'the Eye of the Needle', and this process can only be undertaken in absolute humility and nakedness. You are not allowed to take anything with you. All attachments and spiritual concepts need to dissolve, otherwise they will act as a hindrance, blocking true progress on your journey towards Oneness.

Source has many layers, which is not well known on this planet, for very few human beings have ever reached these higher levels of initiation and merged into Oneness with Source. In order to pass through all of these layers, you have to be willing to be absolutely nothing and nobody. Otherwise you will remain at the level of consciousness you have attained — until you are prepared to let go of all images, spiritual concepts and self importance, for all of this is illusion. Only the ones who are willing to be nothing can be given 'the Crown of Life', and then 'the Secrets of Creation' will be revealed to them. This is a long and at times arduous and testing journey, which cannot be rushed. Countless preparations throughout many lifetimes are required for a soul to be ready to take these sacred steps.

We do not perceive time as you do, and in the higher worlds there is no competition. Everyone progresses according to their own capabilities and this is how it is intended. Is a child in kindergarten on earth able to understand the history lessons at university? Certainly not. The same applies to younger souls, who are simply unable to comprehend the movements and motivations of a more experienced soul in training for spiritual mastership. Do not even try to assess the level of consciousness of someone else if you have not achieved enlightenment, for only then will you be able to see with the eyes of love the true light in your brothers and sisters. Only love will remain and judgment will no longer be an attitude of yours. Remember, only an Avatar can recognise an Avatar. Until you have reached this stage of absolute union with the Divine, do not assess others. There is enough work to be done on your own inner journey, and this is where your attention needs to be focused.

Let us look further into the spiritual path after awakening. You will observe that there are stages of consciousness where you feel like you are dissolving into the light and truly know yourself as an eternal divine being. These experiences of heightened consciousness interchange with times of feeling quite ordinary and disconnected. At this particular point, some of you might believe that they have failed, for they feel unable to connect with their divine light. But this is not the case, for it is only a stage of your journey where you again have to look within and dissolve deeper layers, preventing you from permanently embodying the light.

This is a natural and necessary part of the process. So do not be harsh on yourself when you feel disconnected from the Divine, even after the extraordinary spiritual experience of your initial awakening. This is the only way the Divine can reveal to you what is still living in the darkness of your inner underground. Simply look in wonder and with the curiosity of a child playing. Cleanse and heal these aspects with the help of the Divine, so that the light can fill, overtake and fully inhabit you. Step by step the remaining resistance towards the light will lessen, until one day there is nothing opposing love, peace and truth in every single moment of your existence.

Then you will breathe in and exhale love wherever you are, regardless of what is happening, and see no difference between the events you previously judged as good or bad. Life continues to unfold in waves, but pure consciousness remains untouched. You are one with the light; you are light — enlightened. You will clearly hear the voice of stillness, our voice, wherever you are and everywhere you go. You will be one with your Creator and begin to realise the Oneness with all creation, which is an experience beyond what human words are capable of describing.

Never before in your known history and since the end of the Golden Age have so many souls been ready to awaken. Some have already experienced their initial awakening and are in preparation to master the difficult steps to enlightenment. Your enlightenment will enlighten your brothers and sisters. Remember, everything you do, you do for you as well as for your fellow humans on earth. Your liberation will also become a catalyst for the enlightenment of this beautiful planet and catapult humanity into the next Golden Age. What a joyful and exciting time it is to be with you at the threshold of this sacred transition.

41

DISCERNMENT OF ENERGIES

We would like to share with you our thoughts regarding the discernment of energies. As you might know, there are the Forces of Light serving the Divine — the Light of the One and there are on the other hand, forces that appear to oppose the light and are consequently known as evil or the Forces of Darkness. On earth, you live in a complex system of duality, where between these two opposing poles your life plays out, whether you are aware of this fact or not. In truth, the darkness is not the opposite of the Light, for the Light has no opposite, but it appears this way to the uninitiated. Love or the Light has no opposite. That which you name evil is only the denial of the Light — the absence of Love.

On your planet you can find people such as Mother Theresa and others like Hitler, to mention two well-known but extreme representatives of these opposing polarities. You are also able to meet anyone in between on this vast spectrum of duality. These polarities are set in place to serve you. They are there so that you can use your gift of free will in order to develop discernment. Just imagine: if there was only the light, what choice would you have?

We wish to introduce you to a provocative statement: 'The darkness ultimately always serves the light'. At first glance this sentence sounds contrary to everything you have been taught to believe. So let us help you understand the deeper meaning of this assertion. We are not stating that the darkness intentionally serves the light. You will only be able to gain a deeper understanding of this principle if you are willing to see with the eyes of love. Let us use an example for further clarification: suppose you have been blackmailed or have experienced an emotional attack and you still feel the pain of this event. Instead of choosing the victim role, blaming others and dwelling on self-pity, you could feel and examine your pain. You might discover a part you have abandoned or judged. Now is the time to free this aspect from its inner dungeon and reunite it with your greater self, by applying the simple healing technique taught in the previous chapters.

1. Acknowledge the pain this particular part of you experiences. Own it and send love, understanding and compassion.
2. Ask this inner aspect what are its needs.
3. Connect to the Divine and ask for healing light to be sent to your unloved aspects.

Repeat this process as often as you feel it is necessary, until true integration and healing has happened.

If you choose to turn painful situations into healing opportunities and learn to perceive life through the eyes of your soul, you will step by step become more whole. This was what we meant when we said that the darkness serves the light.

Your soul knows what is real, whereas the human mind easily gets entangled in the illusion of duality. The challenge life presents, is to look through this hologram of polarities and see its illusionary character. Only love is real. Therefore, in the end, the darkness enables you to become aware of your own darkness. When you have resolved all separation thinking, realised the Oneness of all beings, you will no longer react in an unconscious manner towards outer events. Instead you will remain peacefully centred at all times. In truth, in a deeper sense, the task of the darkness is to show you your own darkness and where more inner work is needed.

There is another aspect of the dark energies that we would like to share with you — the discernment between light and dark energies when you meditate or work with energy for healing. We observe a lot of naivety and ignorance regarding this issue, which is of concern. So let us examine the difference between the forces of the light and darkness.

When you open up to the light, you will feel a beautiful warmth and inner peace. Even if you discover one of your unhealed aspects, there will be no judgment: you will only feel unconditionally loved and accepted. The light may appear in many different forms, sometimes gentle and on other occasions powerful, yet you will always sense compassion, heart expansion and a higher view of reality. Your body's sensation might be warm; and the light, although strong, has a soft healing quality. The forces that serve the Divine neither wish to inflate your ego nor will they try to impress you with grandeur or glamour.

When you connect with Source, you will experience peace, love, humility, devotion and surrender. In contrast, whether unintentionally or intentionally, when you come into contact with the dark forces you might encounter the temptation of great power and grandeur being offered to you. This kind of energy may sometimes feel like a stinging sensation in your physical body, sharp or cold, even to the point where your heart contracts. The dark forces might be trying to impress you with glamour and illusion — be aware that there is not only material glamour, but also spiritual glamour. The latter is the more dangerous version of glamour, that can be observed in various spiritual and religious groups. We hope that this short description of the differences between the light and the darkness may help you to find your first steps in learning about the discernment of energies.

Before every meditation or healing session please facilitate a protection ritual. If you should experience the effects of the dark forces in meditation or during a healing, ask immediately for protection. All spiritual teachings from around the world have prayers and rituals for protection that work profoundly. We will introduce a few to you. If you cannot find one from our list of suggestions, you can search your own particular religious or spiritual path for one that suits you:

1. Call in Archangel Michael for protection to create a sphere of light to surround you.
2. Pray the Lord's Prayer and repeat it until you feel safe.
3. Say the Hebrew words: Kodoish, Kodoish, Kodoish Adonai Zebayoth.
4. Ask God, the Divine Mother, the Divine, Source, Allah, Christ or Buddha for the light of protection and ask them to send these negative energies away.

After you have completed your protection ritual, ask for purification from these negative energies. Repeat this meditation until you have cleared your field and are only surrounded by pure divine light. Depending on the force of the psychic attack you have experienced, this cleansing may happen immediately, or it might take a few hours or sometimes days. Never fear the darkness, for if you do, you will give your power away. Remember, darkness feeds on fear. Yet it is important to know about the existence of the dark forces and not to underestimate their power. However, realise that the divine light is always stronger than the forces of darkness. If you have experienced an encounter with the dark energies, examine how and why it has happened. As your light grows stronger, the darkness becomes more interested in diminishing its shine and these negative energies are there to test you. Every event in life can be perceived as a healing and learning opportunity, including an attack from the darkness.

Always align yourself first with the Divine and ask for protection before you begin to work with energies or meditate. Only in this way can you be sure that you work with the energies you intended. Otherwise, it is as if you would leave your home unlocked when going out and are surprised to find burglars and destruction on your return. No-one with common sense would act in this way. The same rules of precaution apply for your 'psychic house', which is your body's energy field. Living on earth means to live in a world of duality, where both of the opposing forces are present.

There is a particular category of dark beings that are called 'the twilight masters' and some of them pose as angels or enlightened Masters. When they appear to you, you will not feel at peace. There is rather an intense energy accompanied by glamour, sensationalising and temptations of grandeur. Remember not to fear these beings, instead firmly send them away and thank the Divine for the valuable lesson in discernment.

The discernment of energies is a science in itself and the knowledge about this subject is still in the developing stages on earth. We ask that you become more interested in studying this important skill so that you do not connect with a 'master' you did not intend. We observe too many spiritual seekers with little training or no proper spiritual preparation naively opening their psychic fields. Due to this fundamental lack of knowledge and the influence of their wounded aspects, these students fall victim to 'sensational' experiences, which they believe to be spiritual and so become the unfortunate prey of these false masters. Be aware that any craving for self-importance always stems from your unhealed inner aspects. It is time for true healing, and only from there can grounded spirituality be developed. If you aim for the noble goal of true inner freedom with perseverance, patience and sincerity, you will not fail.

We advise you to clear and protect your energy fields daily and continuously work on your emotional healing. When you do this on a regular basis you will not fall prey to dark astral entities.

Before you offer your service to others, study thoroughly and wisely the science of energies — the true spiritual teachings — and develop a daily practice in meditation. Listen to your heart, for your heart knows. Never be impressed by energies that your heart feels uncomfortable with. Learn discernment and walk in love and humility. Remember, the darkness cannot harm you if you have healed the darkness within. In fact, you will then realise that neither the darkness nor your false self is real.

42

PROJECTION

Almost every conflict on earth is caused by the unconscious shadow play of your unhealed inner wounds. As a result, most of you perceive life largely through projection, because it is too painful to experience these aspects directly. Usually, you project your split-off aspects on each other and create a life of fear of one another. Yet in truth you live in fear of your own shadow, and most of your motivations and actions are driven by these unhealed wounds.

The process of projection occurs virtually automatically, for directly facing your own shadow seems too hard to bear. As long as you do not heal, you will remain unable to see other people for who they truly are. Therefore, your view of yourself and others will continue to be tainted by the dark glasses of your own shadow. The majority of inhabitants of this beautiful planet are playing this 'game' by projecting their shadow on each other and in this way creating a variety of poisonous emotions towards their fellow humans, which originate from their own hatred, abandonment, fear and unconscious anger. If no healing is undertaken, you will remain caught up in this unpleasant and harmful illusion — feeling trapped in a world inhabited by fear and danger, where no-one trusts another. This behaviour only supports the conviction that you are separate from Source, for negative emotions disconnect you from your divine self.

The truth is there are no enemies, only people who do not know love, who do not love themselves and therefore cannot love their fellow man. Only hurt people hurt. When you are under any form of attack, know that the other person initiating such action only does this out of fear and is unable to truly see himself or you. So do not take negative behaviour towards yourself too personally, for in truth harmful actions of others largely stem from their own inner discomfort and disharmony. When you are in such a situation, always look first at yourself, feel and interrogate if there is any truth in what was said. If something occupies you for longer than ten minutes, know it also has to do with you, whether that means there are insights to gain or corrections to make, or inner healing is needed. Never let pride get in the way and prevent you from growing. When you have no reaction in a confrontation and are able to remain centred and calm, this is an indicator that you have already cured your inner receptor point. In fact, you receive through this situation a confirmation that the healing process of this particular issue is complete.

The Divine teaches every human being through the occurrences in their daily lives. If you fully understand this to be true and ask the question every day, 'What can I learn from this situation or this person coming into my life', your spiritual path will accelerate and you will find yourself on the highway to heaven. Yet this approach to life requires continuous inner work and your full attention, to prevent you from slipping back into projection, blaming others or losing yourself in negative emotions. This is a major step in the process of reversing your main conditioning. You will exchange projection, blame and fear with love, compassion, deep insight, healing and true understanding. A useful and necessary tool on this path is to become 'the observer' of your own emotions, thoughts and actions. Without this valuable tool it will be difficult to succeed.

Your willingness to heal on a personal and collective level is your only chance to enter this new age of peace — the age of brotherhood and sisterhood on earth. In general, what you believe to be true about someone else is, in the majority of cases, not real. You cannot change another person; you can only change yourself. In following this rule you will raise your frequency, and your life will transform miraculously. It seems to be a common occupation on your planet to entertain yourself with great seriousness in the business of changing someone else. Nearly all of these attempts fail and result in resentment and frustration. Why do you not give up such pointless and energy-consuming behaviour and direct your focus towards yourself? The only person you can truly change and be responsible for is you. In fact, this is the precise job description of everyone's life on earth.

Study the secret meaning of the symbol of the Spiral. Everything begins at its innermost core and spirals from the inside out. You inner world is the centre and your spiritual life is the foundation for everything that exists in your life. This law applies for you personally as well as collectively. What you perceive as problems and difficulties in the outer world are only the reflections or consequences of the disharmony of your inner life. Consequently, it is a waste of breath to complain about the world. You can only find solutions for the problems in your society when you start from within. First, heal yourself, for only the one who lives in love and harmony with himself is able to make loving and mature decisions that will have a positive impact on the world.

If enough people change their lives and heal themselves, your world will automatically heal and you will see for the first time the light of your True Self as well as the beauty of others, which has been hidden for so long.

43

FORGIVENESS

Dear friends, let us examine a subject that is very dear to us — forgiveness. We observe that many of you do not know how to forgive, nor do you comprehend the consequences of non-forgiveness on your life and that of others. We see places within you where you do not dare to go and feel unable to confront, for there lie deep shame, guilt, pain and fear. You rather choose to live with these very uncomfortable emotions than to look at them honestly and with love, understanding and compassion. These hidden emotions act like infested wounds, poisoning and preventing you from finding true inner freedom. Once you are ready and willing to examine these dark corners within, you will realise that avoiding these uncomfortable emotions is actually more painful than taking a clear look at what has caused your self-judgment, guilt and shame. We encourage all of you to confront your deepest pain, for only then can true healing occur.

For example, you may feel from your current perspective that you have acted wrongly in the past. This could be anything from dishonesty or betrayal to a point where your behaviour is considered a crime by law. What happens in the moment when you realise that you have done something wrong? You may feel regret, shame, guilt, possibly even horror towards your actions and yourself. Harsh self-judgment would be your most likely reaction. You may have thoughts and convictions that are unconsciously deeply rooted in your whole being, such as 'I can never forgive myself', 'I am not worth anything', 'I have not earned the right for any good to happen to me after what I have done' or similar negative statements. These sentences are etched into your subconscious and carry a high emotional charge. They almost have the same effect as a vow and can limit the expansion of your consciousness for many lifetimes.

Even if you are unaware of their powerful impact, you will still create your life experiences according to these limiting convictions, setting yourself up for failure and self-sabotage, for unconsciously you believe in their negative messages and send out a matching vibration. Without your knowing, these negative beliefs will influence all events in your life. Their power is such that you will experience what you believe, and these beliefs will be confirmed through negative and painful events that will manifest in your life, for manifestation follows thought.

The guilt, shame, regret and self-punishment you feel today can often be traced back to events and actions that happened long ago, perhaps hundreds or even thousands of years. Begin unearthing the true cause of these emotions, understand and forgive yourself. Only then will you heal your pain. Until you have learned to forgive yourself, you will remain unable to fully align with your true nature. Everything, including all fear, shame, guilt, self-judgment, hatred and jealousy, has to be brought into the light — to the altar of the Divine — if you wish to become an expression of your true nature. The Divine knows all aspects of you and is not judging you. So it is about you truly getting to know yourself and transforming everything that is not in love *into* love — and forgive all that is judged.

Most of you believe that you have a few acceptable, good and beautiful attributes and there are aspects you would prefer to hide — even from yourself. The Divine sees what you are trying to hide and encourages you to embrace all of you, even the aspects you consider to be the worst, such as the coward, the greedy one, the one who wants blind revenge and the part in you which is in so much fear that it is only able to think of its own advantage. At first, this embrace may feel awkward and uncomfortable, but it is the only way to true healing and necessary for the re-education of these imbalanced inner aspects.

It is important to acknowledge that all human beings act from their current level of consciousness and that most of you do your best according to your knowledge and awareness. You might be familiar with the situation where you look back at specific events in your life that happened many years ago and think 'Oh my God, how could I have been so naive' or 'I would have acted differently given my time again'. You feel this way because your consciousness and viewpoint have changed and you have developed a more mature and deeper understanding of life. In fact, you are no longer the same person. We do not say that your shadow part is not in need of correction, but improving negative behaviour is only possible through deep inner healing, love, understanding and compassion for oneself. Judging yourself and abandoning some of these aspects, metaphorically speaking, can be compared on an energetic level to holding an umbrella above your head, preventing the sun — the light of the Divine — to shine on you.

We would like to show you the consequences of being unable to forgive yourself, thus allowing these inner convictions, created by the deep remorse of your past behaviour, to continue to strongly influence your life. These sentences are very powerful and live as an undercurrent within you, controlling and sabotaging everything you do. These convictions will continue to manifest and become your reality. For instance, if you unconsciously believe 'I can never forgive myself' or 'I do not deserve anything good to happen to me, after what I have done', through 'the law of attraction' you will draw events into your life reflecting these beliefs. Unfortunately, continued confirmation of these negative convictions will develop an even stronger acceptance within you that these beliefs are the truth. As a result, your own hatred and self-judgment will increase. At the same time, anger will arise, as you experience the negative effects of your beliefs. You will find yourself powerless, switching back and forth between judgment and anger, as well as feeling a mixture of resentment and resignation, convinced that you have not earned better.

Although these negative convictions may have been created long ago, they nevertheless act just as effectively in your subconscious, which holds all of your emotional records. The reason for your underlying self-sabotage remains invisible, for the majority of human beings are unable to remember past lives, yet the emotions causing this unpleasant situation survived throughout the centuries. It is not necessary for everyone to have past-life regression therapy, although it can support you on your journey to wholeness. Yet you will all find deep negative convictions from the past resurfacing in this life. Find the most judgmental sentence sabotaging your life and then bring light and compassion to this inner aspect that suffered under your own mercilessness. Then ask the Divine for help to heal this abandoned and despised inner part.

From our viewpoint, self-judgment, even though it is very common among human beings, makes little sense and is entirely counterproductive. This negative behaviour only confirms your sense of unworthiness and cages you between anger and victim mentality, both of which are limiting illusionary perceptions of yourself, holding you in a vicious cycle. All negative sentiments close you off from Source, whereas emotions founded in love, truth and peace connect you with the Divine.

So what do you do when you realise that your actions were wrong? Instead of embarking on the usual self-loathing, turn immediately to the light for healing of the aspects that have led to this negative behaviour. If not, you will only continue with the old path, pushing yourself further into darkness and significantly lengthening your journey home. The Divine does not treat you in this way, so why do you punish yourself? Your Creator always forgives, even before the act is done, and opens his heart for you to receive love. God *is* forgiveness. In the Worlds of Light there exists no punishment. There is only the offer of love, understanding, mercy and compassion. Let the Divine teach you how to forgive, be patient and have mercy and compassion, and so develop deep understanding for yourself and others. Go within the innermost core of your sacred heart and connect with your divine light. In the stillness beyond silence, you will find guidance and support.

When you have truly learnt to forgive yourself, you will be able to forgive others. Remember, very rarely does a human being intentionally harm another. The majority of you act as well as they are able, according to their level of consciousness.

If someone has wronged and hurt you, find your reacting part. You might experience a variety of intense emotions when you have not been acknowledged or have been disrespected, wrongly criticised, blackmailed, lied to, betrayed or robbed of your property. In the end it does not matter what the reason is for these feelings; what is truly important is how you deal with them. Embrace the hurting aspect in you, love it and have compassion and understanding. Reflect on how you treat yourself: perhaps the other person is only an outer mirror of your inner merciless judge. Ask the question 'Do I respect, support and stand behind myself, or do I abandon and criticise myself constantly and act with disrespect towards my own needs, believing unconsciously that I have not earned better. If you truly listen, you will be able to find an answer, providing you with great opportunities for inner growth.

When your healing of this particular aspect is complete, you can then focus your attention on forgiving the other person in this scenario. You will be surprised to discover that, as your healing is completed, forgiving will come naturally, whereas before it appeared to be almost unthinkable, for you were reacting from your inner wound. You will know that you are healed when you feel filled with love — a vessel overflowing. Love and forgiveness are the side effects of true inner healing. Be patient, for everything is a process. The more you practise, the more you will come to realise that in truth there is nothing to forgive, only more to love within yourself and in others. Remember, if you do not forgive, you are denying God's love and light within you, for we are all One. In fact, the person you are hurting the most is yourself.

44

GRACE

If you were able to live in complete 'Yes-ness' to life, you would not be in need of the healing steps explained throughout this book. This 'Yes' to life would align you instantly with your divinity, and your limited beliefs and fears would no longer have control over you. In fact this 'Yes' to life is the highway to heaven. Say 'Yes' to all of you, as well as all outer circumstances and events, and accept them as your chance to remember who you are. Then you will dance freely on earth, unimpressed by the phantoms of fear. Beloveds, this is a great secret that we reveal to you. It is for the ones who have a humble, childlike heart and a still mind — it is the remedy for all illness in your world. You are troubled, for you believe more in fear and limitation than you believe in God's love for you, which is able to create miracles.

Let us use the example of someone receiving a diagnosis of a serious life-threatening illness. Most of you would focus entirely on the horrendous consequences this sickness might have in the future, instead of putting your attention on what you desire to be — healthy, joyful, alive, safe and peaceful. You know that your thoughts are creating your reality. Can you imagine the disastrous effect of these fearful and hopeless thought forms? On the other hand, imagine if you were able to accept the diagnosis and immediately focus on your perfect health, beginning with the cleansing of your body and strengthening yourself on every level. You would only do more of the things that make you happy, content and peaceful.

You might decide to commence the advised treatment of your medical doctors with additional alternative healing and supplementation, but with a clear and positive mind and without the all-so-commonly-experienced fear. You would put your whole attention towards seeing and feeling yourself as already healed and act in the deep trust and knowing of the divine light that you are. Your main focus would be on your connection to the Divine, for you recognise that the light of Source is perfect, all-powerful, totally harmonious and absolutely in balance. Through meditation and prayer you would draw this pure light into your whole being, immersing all of your cells in its radiance in order to restore inner balance, healing and harmony. You would know that the disharmony and imbalance that created this illness cannot maintain its presence in your physical body when you make space for the healing power of your Creator. You are all energy: all of your various subtle bodies are energy on different levels of vibration and manifestation.

Source is pure love, the highest energy in creation. If you truly allow the Divine to completely overtake you and merge with your whole being, nothing that is out of order or in disharmony can remain so. All have to obey. All of your cells — your whole being — will obey this higher divine order and rearrange accordingly and heal. This is the law. Yet, because the majority of humanity do not trust God, and do not even consider the possibility of direct contact with their Creator, this wonderful offer is seldom accepted.

Occasionally some inexplicable healings occur and you call them miracles. The reason for this may have been due to this leap from fear to total trust — an acceptance of everything that is, this 'yes' to life. This point of inner surrender is symbolised by the open lotus flower, beloveds — the absolute 'yes-ness' to life as it is, in the full knowing that you are loved and taken care of under all circumstances. This giant leap can only occur through deep trust in divine grace, which seems today to be an old-fashioned and outdated concept. Nevertheless, the promise of divine grace is still at hand for all of you. You only have to believe, trust and open up to it.

Unfortunately, the western mind is not very receptive to our offer and usually puts it aside as a redundant notion, only relevant in spiritual tales of the long-forgotten past. Yet nothing has changed; God's offer is still the same. The simple-minded people in ancient times were more open to this offer, whereas the sophistication of your modern, educated mind rejects it. It is your beliefs that have changed; your Creator never changes. You try to limit that which is unlimited with your beliefs, but in the end you only limit yourself.

We want you to believe again in miracles. We want you to dream for the possibility of the impossible. We want you to become the children you have once been. Did Jesus not say that if you do not become like little children, you cannot enter his kingdom? This is the truth, and it still applies today. Call upon God's grace, come and talk to the Divine like a child. Lay all of your worries and difficulties on the altar of your heart and leave them there. The Divine will take care of them. So many of you have created a distant God, a non-existent God, a God for whom you have to be perfect for him to listen, an unreachable God, a God only for the chosen ones. We are here today to tell you that all of this is *your* creation and has nothing to do with your Creator. We are love, forgiveness, peace, truth; we are always here for you in every moment of your life. In fact, God lives inside of you. You are a part of the Supreme Being to whom you gave the name God, the Divine Mother, Allah, the Creator and so many other names. You are divine, and it is time to claim your heritage.

Throw away the concepts that separate you from the Source of all being. Call upon divine grace. Call upon help, guidance, support and comfort. Call upon healing and your prayer will be heard. The vast energy you call God is All That Is, which includes you and all of creation, and is able to do anything. Do you believe The Nameless One that gave all of you your names and created all universes, the formless and the form, the visible and the invisible, would not be able to correct some inner imbalances in your body, which you call illness? It is *you* who has to make the shift in thinking to allow miracles to happen. You need to become like the children when you wish to enter the kingdom of God. You keep yourself outside the doors of heaven by believing in sickness, unsolvable problems and difficulties, rather than inviting the Divine into your life. Invite us into everything you do and every breath you take, with childlike trust.

Take responsibility for yourself, align with your true inner essence and leave the rest up to the Divine. This is 'Heaven on Earth'. Your future generations will act upon this advice. Pave the way for them, by trusting that the Divine cares and takes care. Let go of the control your mind desires and begin to trust your heart, which is our connection. Divine grace will shower upon you. It may take a different form to what you expect, but if you truly look with the eyes of your soul you will clearly detect God's signature beginning to manifest in your life. Come with everything troubling you to your inner sacred altar, lay down your burdens and ask for divine intervention and guidance. You will see your life turning around in the most unexpected ways.

You must first understand that all is possible for the Divine and, because you are a part of the Divine, all is possible for you. This is our promise! You only need to fully surrender to the Divine — the light that lives within you.

45

GOD IS EVERYWHERE

God is everywhere. Nothing exists where God is not present as the inherent life-giving force. There would be no life without the Divine. You would not exist, neither would the trees, plants, animals nor any form of life or the vastness of all universes with their star systems and suns. We watch so many of you searching for God, but your God is a concept and you overlook the light and love of God that is within and all around you, beloveds. God smiles at you through the sun and touches you through the wind, another human being, the scent of a flower, the innocent play of your child and the silent whispers of your heart. Most of the time you are unable to recognise God's communication with you and instead look for enlightenment in spiritual practices, tailored to your convictions and concepts, a search that seldom leads to success. We wish to remind you of the ancient and eternal truth — that God is available and reachable every second of your life, if you are prepared to cast off your concepts and beliefs about the Divine.

Another important condition for our conscious connection is your willingness to empty yourself from your identification with your ego self and the resulting attachments that keep you bound to limitation. As long as you are full of ideas of who you are and how to reach God, the true light of wisdom cannot be given, nor will you experience the sacred union with All That Is.

When you look at a glass filled with wine, how can this glass ever become a vessel for pure water? First you must empty the glass and then thoroughly clean it, so that no residue of the wine remains. Only then will your vessel become a clear, untainted chalice. It is the same with your True Self (water) and your false self or mask (wine). As long as you identify with your ego self and its projection, defence and hurt, you will be unable to recognise your oneness with the Divine. You need to completely empty yourself to experience this sacred union.

If you believe that spirituality is limited to prayer, meditation and the study of spiritual teachings, we have to correct you. Spirituality is everything you do and how you do it. How you water your garden, how you treat your work colleagues, your partner, your children, the people who do not love you and so on. The distinction you formulate between what you consider to be spiritual and what you believe is only the mundane part of life will fall away in the future of the New Earth. People will recognise that true spirituality involves everything in life — the way they treat themselves and others, how they conduct their businesses and deal with complex decisions, how they treat the earth, and what they eat. They will understand that without true spiritual guidance for *everything* in life, they are lost and cut off from Spirit. They will comprehend that they are Spirit and everyone will know the purpose of true life, namely, to become the full expression of their inherent divinity, to spiritualise matter and to materialise their divine light in their daily lives.

The distant God will be considered an old-fashioned, superstitious concept of the past, and no-one will be able to understand how you, the people of the early 21st century, could have sincerely believed in this man-made construct. We call you now to question all of your concepts of the Divine and let them go, for they stand as an obstacle between the Divine and you, preventing our union.

Another long-held belief is that you need a guru to become enlightened. You do not need a guru to give to you the divine light. You are this very light, which became oblivious of its true nature. Despite the fact that you are unable to remember who you are, God is still accessible for each one of you at any moment of your life. You only have to make an effort and apply what you have learned so far. The spiritual journey with a guru is an older model of guidance to the Divine that has its place in the evolution of human consciousness. It has its advantages as it has its flaws. One of the obvious flaws is that the presence of the guru, despite providing valuable guidance, creates a dependency for most disciples, resulting in an unnecessary giving away of personal power.

Understand that all of you are able to connect directly with the Divine without giving your power away to a Master. You do not need a negotiator to communicate with God. God is you! Through ignoring this fundamental truth the worship of the guru was created, whereas in the higher worlds of consciousness only the Divine is praised. The divine light that some of you see in the Master should never become a reason for worship, rather an encouragement to make space for your own divine light.

As long as you are in a physical body you are more or less bound to the illusion of duality and rarely totally free. Why do so many of you make the detour on their spiritual journey and devote themselves to a guru instead of connecting directly with the Divine? The Divine does not need your power or money, will not create an unhealthy dependency, nor will it ever mislead you. We, who are speaking from the Centre of Source, the Heart of God, are calling you to begin your journey of trust in God's Presence in every moment of your life. God is here — right now — and is there for you. Enlightenment cannot be achieved, for it is given by divine grace, when you are empty enough to receive. Get used to love, abundance and peace. Get to know your divine self. God is love, peace, joy, almighty beyond human imagination and at the same time your closest friend. God is you.

Not only do you have to let go of your concept of an unreachable, distant God, you also have to throw out the belief of a God who punishes you for your sins. God is the purest love and has never punished any of his creation. In endless patience and love, the Divine guides you all back into its innermost heart. We deeply wish that you begin to feel God's love for you and that you understand that love is God's true nature. When you truly understand this, all pain will lift from your shoulders and you will comprehend that it is only your limited concepts that are keeping you away from divine union.

In truth, you are moving through the Divine with everything you do. You breathe God because the air is God, you eat God because all food comes from the life-giving energy of the Divine. Everything you touch is God, filled with his spirit; otherwise it could not exist. Everything you see is God, including yourself. If you could fully comprehend what we have just said, you would live in Oneness with everything that is and begin to truly touch the divine mystery. God does not want to be worshipped in your temples. God wants you to worship with everything you do. Be the love you want to see in this world. Love yourself, everyone and everything. Celebrate life; be at peace and live the truth. This is true spirituality, which enables you to fully align with the Divine. Then you may understand that God is exploring God's self through everyone and everything in his creation.

46

GOD DID NOT CREATE EVIL

Beloveds, God did not create evil. All that is created is created by love. How then could anything created by love be evil? What you call evil is created by the same love consciousness as that which you call the ultimate good or the Divine. The only difference is that what you perceive as evil has closed off from love, its origin, whereas what you consider as good is in complete alignment with the Divine. The almighty, unlimited consciousness of the Supreme Being has never created anything evil. It is the decision of its creation to disconnect from its Source.

As a consequence of this choice, light has turned into darkness and love into fear. All negativity in this vast creation only exists for this reason. In endless love and patience, the Supreme Being allows all of its creation to make its own choices and experience itself as separate and therefore limited. These experiences range from absolute Oneness with the Divine to almost complete separation, and they determine the content of light, which equals love — or the degree of darkness and fear in a soul. Since evil was never created by the Divine, our wish is for you to understand the enormity of choice that the Divine is allowing its creation. This also shows the endless trust and love of the Divine for its creation.

We who are embodying divine love, the Heart of God, would like to share as much as is possible in human words about the love your Creator has for all of creation, for love is rarely understood on your planet. We would like to give you a taste of God's love. God is All That Is. This includes all beings that have shut themselves off from the Divine and act out of self-centredness, fear and distrust, and crave for superficial power. Despite their negative behaviour, the Divine loves them the same way as you would love your drug-addicted child who has lost his way in life. God loves the ones who have fallen into darkness just as he loves the ones serving the light. All of creation carries the divine spark of light — is God's child — is God — and therefore able to completely unite with him and be like him: almighty, all-powerful, never-ending love and peace. This spark only needs to be reignited and nurtured through surrender to the Supreme Being. Yet the return to the light can only occur in absolute free will if it is to succeed. We wish to let you — who are God's creation — feel God's love, whether you are aligned with the light or have turned away from it.

The Divine loves all of you, regardless of your level of consciousness. Love pours out to all of creation, just as the rays of the sun touch the weeds in the same way as the beautiful flowers and fruits to give them life force. Just as the sun does not discriminate between weeds and the so-called useful plants, in the same manner God does not withhold his love. The Supreme Being is love itself in its purest essence, far and beyond human words are capable of describing — love loving itself through all of its creation, holding all of you forever in its embrace. This is what the Heart of God does and has done since the beginning of time.

You might ask why we are telling you this. Well, the main reason why you are on earth is to rediscover that you are love. Your planet is called by some 'the planet of fear', which is why you are able to learn love so well in this environment of apparent polarity. In sharing our love — the Creator's love for you — we wish to encourage you to invoke God's love and learn to love everyone and everything in the same way as God loves you. Through opening up to love, you are becoming love again, which is what you have always been. Some of you might believe that you need to learn love. But we would like to tell you a secret — you do not need to learn anything. Simply make space for your divine part, which is already everything you have ever wanted to be, in absolute balance, divine perfection and abundance. You are love, you are divine — even the darkest of beings. If you send love to what you consider to be evil, you will remind the dark beings of their forgotten origin and help to reignite their divine light.

One day, all of creation will return to Source, reunite with its Creator and become aware of its own divinity. This is universal law, and neither resistance nor denial of your divine light can prevent your return. You can compare this process with the analogy of a strong magnet pulling metal towards it. The metal can try as hard as it wants to resist, but in the end it has to give in because the pull towards the magnet is too strong. This pull is also known as the call of your soul. If a soul receives its inner calling, nothing in your world will ever satisfy this soul again, until the soul unites with Source. A large number of human beings have received this wake-up call during the last few decades and responded, and more are due to receive the calling.

Not since the rise of Atlantis have there been so many of you ready to embark on their spiritual journey and unite with their true selves. The fastest way to reach your destination is love. Be the love you are: love everyone and everything. Remember what we said at the beginning of this chapter — your Creator has created everything in love. God is love. What you call evil, wrong or bad is still in its essence the same love, but has simply forgotten that it is love. Instead of sending hatred to the ones you consider evil, send love. This will remind them of what they have forgotten. Step by step, if enough of you are practising love, those living oblivious to their true nature will begin to remember. Love is the fastest way to God and into everyone's heart. We, the Heart of God, love you — since ever and forever. Remember, people only act cruelly if they are cruel to themselves. Only their mask is cruel; beneath, in their essence, they are still the shining light that is divine.

One of the messages for the New Earth is that you do not need religions that instil a sense of unworthiness in you or declare you to be born sinners. The religious concept of evil is only a reflection of your own human unloved parts and their outer projection. These long-held false beliefs will fall away in the near future. You will recognise your own divinity as well as the divinity of each other, and realise that you are love — divine and inherently good. Only fear and pain created your artificial mask and limited personality. In the end, even religions are only products of this mask and inner limitations, and their rules are purely human interpretations of the divine laws, which in these circumstances were severely misunderstood. One day you will all comprehend that what you call God is love — and you will open up to this love when your time has come.

God is all and everything. Nothing exists but God. Nothing exists that is not God, which is also true for you. You will realise that the old religious concepts were only reflecting a deeply ingrained human self-hatred, denial and limitation. In the near future you will be able to set the record straight, peel back the layers of misunderstanding and false human interpretations of the universal laws, and return to the true essence of all spiritual teachings, which have existed since eternity. You will then understand that what all religions tried to capture in so many different ways were always the same divine laws taught throughout all cultures and civilisations — known, unknown and long forgotten — and you will realise the simple truth that you are divine — one with God. *You are Love!* Love just as the Supreme Being loves everything and everyone, and the sacred mysteries of creation will be revealed to you.

47

NEW LEADERSHIP VERSUS AUTOCRATIC LEADERSHIP

What you are experiencing at the moment is the beginning of the shift from autocratic leadership to a true living democracy birthing itself from the inside out. This shift is one of the reasons why you are confronted with so much uncertainty, chaos and unpredictability. Concepts and structures that you could rely on for so long have ceased to be effective and useful. There is an underlying impression that you can no longer count on anything. In this context it is helpful to remember that change is the very nature of life, and that you are in the middle of a major shift in human consciousness. So let us go into further detail and examine what this imminent transformation of consciousness means in relation to your leaders and leadership in general.

You are witnessing the end of autocratic leadership and its old-style leaders. Autocratic leadership necessitates that there is one who rules and all others follow his lead and advice. It also means that this type of leader holds an almost omnipotent power, whether imagined or not, to which everyone else has to submit. Old-style leaders are generally not interested in the self-empowerment of their fellow man, for this process is considered dangerous to their invincible style of rulership. Well, it is not only that this category of leader is not interested in empowering their people — we need to go as far as saying that they try at all costs to prevent this fundamental shift from happening. The reason for their fear and resistance to change is relatively easy to identify: if everyone else was in his own power, autocratic leadership would no longer work. Empowering others would mean the end of their present leadership style. Whether consciously or unconsciously, every old-style autocratic leader is aware of this danger.

For some time now you have been witnessing the beginning of the crumbling of the old power structures. It does not matter where you direct your attention, the signs of deterioration are visible in all areas of your personal, social, religious and political landscapes — you will detect some form of change in all of these facets of daily life. The nature of change is uncertainty, temporary chaos, leading to the search for new strategies and goals. In the end you will witness the emergence of a new understanding. When you consider how much time personal transformation takes, you will gain a realistic impression of how lengthy, difficult and time-consuming this shift in mass consciousness will be with regard to global political, social and religious structures.

Now consider this: You are already at the beginning of this enormous change, which will not leave anything or anyone unquestioned. It is important to pause at this point and read the previous sentence again. We said, 'You are at the beginning …' This is where we want to direct your attention. This process of transformation has now begun, which means that many of you already find yourselves in the crucial phase of chaos and uncertainty. Is this not what most of you are experiencing?

This is a radical global as well as personal transformation, and you need to comprehend that this change will take its course in its own time. True patience is required. Being well informed will also be of value to support you through this time of chaos and uncertainty. When you develop inner awareness, even if the situation feels painful and inconvenient, this new knowledge will assist in supporting the necessary process of transformation. Whereas, if you have no understanding of what is going on, it is more likely that you will become overwhelmed by fear. This is why we make our voice audible to the world — for we know that, when you comprehend the deeper meaning of this shift, the unavoidable chaos that is a natural by-product of change will instill less fear in you.

We have already mentioned that all autocratic styles of leadership will cease. You can also observe this change in your personal relationships, where the man is no longer automatically the head of a family. For the last few decades, women have been standing up for equal rights and have achieved enormous gains, at least in the western countries. This momentous change has influenced the way women and men relate to each other. A woman of today no longer needs to stay in a loveless marriage purely for economic reasons, for her education now enables her to look after herself financially. The social inequality between a soul incarnated in a male or female body is at last finding its long-awaited balance.

Let us focus on another area: your religious landscape, where two generations ago major power was still held. This power is now visibly fading. The cause for this decline in power is manyfold. Let us look at one reason, which is your longing for a true connection with the Divine and the opportunity and freedom to question established beliefs. Only a few decades ago this behaviour would have been labelled as blasphemy and social isolation and judgment would have been the brutal consequence. Let us go back a few centuries where you would have lost your life simply for having the audacity to doubt or question the religious doctrines.

Now let us examine your political arena. Again, a century ago, dictatorial political systems were common throughout the world. In contrast, the majority of countries have today adopted the principles of democracy and the ones which have not, face internal resistance. The deep longing of humanity for equality and freedom of thought and speech, as well as basic human rights, is becoming more evident. Lately, we have observed in some of the leading nations, the rise of populism. The voters of this kind of leader are longing for a strong father figure to safely guide them through this time of uncertainty and protect them from chaos. Yet, these populistic leaders will not remain in power for long for they embody the outgoing model of leadership.

Humanity as a whole is waking up from a system of suppression that has ruled them for thousands of years. Why is this so? Why now?

The reason for this change is your change in consciousness. Remember, you are creating your world. A substantial part of humanity refuses to remain in victim consciousness. All over the world, human beings are raising their voices in relation to issues of injustice and oppression. They have begun to believe in their right to live in peace and freedom and to enjoy general wellbeing. It is fear that is holding oppressive systems in place, and letting go of fear initiates change. Fear released on a group-consciousness level is bringing on the present change.

We would like to give another example to illustrate this fundamental global shift. The business world is greatly affected by this transformation. Until recent times the old-style boss was not questioned as being an essential and necessary part of a successful business model. This has changed. Autocratic leadership, where the leader has poor listening and communication skills, is acknowledged as one of the leading causes of corporate collapse and failure, globally. If business leaders do not adopt the new style of leadership, based on empowerment for all employees and an inner purpose statement, these businesses will no longer have a future. On the New Earth, business leaders will encourage all of their employees to develop their own creativity, take greater responsibility and become involved in spiritual and emotional development, simply because they will know that content and self-empowered employees are the biggest asset of a company. The business leader of the future will not control and manipulate his people, nor will he keep them in fear. Instead, he will guide and work with them in an environment of mutual respect and trust.

Leaders of the New Earth, whether in the political or business sphere, will need to undertake thorough spiritual and educational training as well as emotional healing before they will be able to provide balanced guidance. They will honour the people who work with them and ask for their input and ideas when appropriate. There will be an equal relationship, and artificial fear-based hierarchies will disappear from the face of the earth.

The old system of autocracy will fall and be replaced by true democracy and guidance from your Higher Self. The new leaders will encourage others to access their true power and full potential. These leaders will not act from fear; instead they will live in trust and alignment with the Divine, knowing that if everyone is in their true power the whole will benefit. Thus they will do everything necessary to support the healing and awakening of their people. In contrast, the old autocratic leaders fear nothing more than others coming into their own power, for this would endanger their position. In fact, this is one of the major differences between these two styles of leadership. The old-style leader fears the true power of others and will prevent them from moving into their own power, whereas the new leader will do his utmost to encourage them. One leadership style is based on fear and the other is founded on love and trust. Which boss would you choose?

As we are examining leadership styles of the past, present and future, we should not forget to take a deeper look at spiritual and religious leadership. Spiritual leadership, whether in traditional religions or other spiritual groups, is also often marked by autocratic leadership styles. It is therefore not surprising to discover that the majority of followers of these groups are giving their power away to their leaders. We consider this behaviour to be dangerous and totally opposed to true spirituality, which connects you to the Divine and allows you to access your true power, grounded in wisdom and love. Unfortunately, many spiritual and religious teachers of the past and present have exhibited unhealthy and damaging behaviour in relation to their leadership style. Because they wish to maintain their position of 'omnipotence', they have no interest in your empowerment and awakening. In actual fact, true empowerment would make their own position redundant. We literally need to go this far and state that these groups and institutions are interested in keeping you in your current state of unconsciousness — dependent, wounded and in fear, and thus willing to give your power away. Hence, we can say that the old-style religious and spiritual groups, with their autocratic leaders, prevent you from becoming whole and actually sabotage true awakening.

The spiritual leaders of the New Earth will be very different. These beautiful beings will guide you to your true nature with respect, wisdom and compassion. Their sole interest will lie in your full empowerment and inner healing. These beings will have passed their initiations and become the living embodiments of what they teach. They will not be interested in being worshiped, nor your emotional dependency. Even though you could call these new spiritual leaders Masters, Saints or even Christs, they will insist on being no more special than anyone else — only there to serve you as your older brothers and sisters. These are the new leaders of the Golden Age. Some of them are already living among you and you will recognise them if you look with the eyes of your heart.

Wonderful times are about to unfold for this planet. Develop patience and understand the significance of what we have shared in relation to the major changes occurring. They will transform earth, ruled by fear for far too long, into the paradise it has been destined to become for eons. Walk your inner journey step by step and trust the unknown. Trust your heart to lead you home. Remind yourself that, after uncertainty and chaos, a new consciousness will emerge, laying the foundation for the New World.

48

THE LIGHT BRINGS UP THE SHADOW

Let us examine another important universal law: The light brings up the shadow. Although this law is at work at all times, as it is a natural function of the light to make the shadow visible, most of you remain unaware of this fundamental law.

When you begin practising spiritual work and meditation, one of your expectations is to attain greater inner peace, and this is often the case. Yet, at times you also experience overwhelming negative emotions surfacing without apparent reason. For instance, you may generally feel content with yourself and your life, but after participating in a spiritual workshop you leave feeling rather confused and experiencing an unknown inner upheaval, instead of finding more peace and love. Why is this so? Since the light cannot bring up your whole shadow at once, it does its work step by step, in accordance with your inner ability to deal with your wounds. Some of you might get confused when these uncomfortable feelings are surfacing and believe something is wrong, for you are convinced that you should only experience peace and love when working with the light.

We need to tell you that you are mistaken with this assumption. Certainly, the light *is* peace and love, but also truth — and truth brings everything into the open that is misaligned with the Divine. Do not become upset when negative emotions are emerging. Know that these feelings have lived within you for a long time and are in need of healing, which is the reason why they are now coming up. Be grateful and place no judgment on your feelings, simply observe them and begin the healing process. It is the natural ability of the light to bring all shadow parts into the open. All that is not light, love, peace and truth will be revealed, for you to heal, integrate and become whole. Do not fear this process; instead welcome these emotions and continue your inner work.

Another common error in thinking is the assumption that when you have participated in various spiritual groups and workshops and developed a regular mediation practise, you consider yourself as 'spiritually advanced' and that there may no longer be any further inner work necessary. This assumption cannot be further from the truth. The spiritual path is a lifelong commitment, learning how to make space for the light and choosing love over fear in every moment. It is important that you realise the inner journey never ends and needs your absolute dedication. It may be difficult for you to comprehend that even the Enlightened Ones are continuously growing and forever expanding in consciousness.

As long as you believe that participating in spiritual workshops, visiting ashrams and meditating will guide you to inner peace, you are on a dangerous road that may well lead you into the sticky spider web of illusion instead of true freedom. This attitude can be compared with someone saying "Well, a year ago I brushed my teeth twice a day for a period of three weeks, and I do not understand why I now have severe pain and tooth decay." Only regular inner cleansing and healing, along with trust, naked honesty, perseverance, patience, inner discipline and choosing love over fear every moment of your life will lead you to your divine self. From this foundation, inspired action will follow, thus changing your life.

All separation, imbalances and fears need to be acknowledged and healed, which include the separation between human and divine, body and spirit, the material and spiritual world, male and female energies and so on. If you truly wish to find freedom, you have to put your spiritual journey first. Your inner path needs to be your priority and come before everything else, which includes your own personal desires and needs, your relationships, career and material belongings. Only then will you reach your goal.

The spiritual journey cannot be lived as a 'holiday experience' or as an entertaining trip. In some circles it seems to have become fashionable to meditate and to be interested in spiritual matters. Yet the spiritual journey is the true purpose of your existence — of everyone's existence — and can only be walked in total surrender. To be 'a little spiritual', but with all of the safety mechanisms and attachments of your material world still in place, will never work. The divine light will reveal all pretences, fears and lies. This is not done to expose or shame you, rather to heal you, for the Divine loves you. It is God's love for you making your shortcomings visible, for as long as they remain hidden beneath the surface and linger in your unconscious, there will be no chance for liberation and healing. This is the reason why the light brings up the shadow. It is God's love for you. Remember, the path of transformation never ends. There is always more to learn, to love and to surrender to. Slow is the growth towards perfection.

49

LIGHT VERSUS DARKNESS

Let us turn our attention to another topic: the path of the light versus the path of darkness. The distinction between these fundamentally different pathways is rarely fully understood, and we find that there is an elemental lack of clarity and discernment with regard to what sets them apart.

Let us first investigate the specifics of the path of darkness. Generally, a student of the occult is fascinated by paranormal and psychic phenomena and feels that there is more to life than just what he sees with his eyes and is tangible. This is often how this journey commences, which is similar to the beginning of the path of an earnest spiritual seeker of the divine light. From this point, however, these two journeys drift quickly apart. The occult path is led by curiosity about the invisible without the acknowledgment of the student's emotional, mental and physical imbalances and their need for healing. Often the focus is solely on the accumulation of knowledge and the investigation of the invisible worlds. The beginner, as with all human beings who have not been engaged in substantial inner healing work, lives entirely directed by the ego self, which is created by his wounds, causing him to build an artificial persona as protection from pain and suffering. Because the student is unconscious of his own inner state of being, he progresses on his journey without opening up to love — the Divine — and therefore remains unbalanced on the emotional and mental levels.

As he continues further on his path, his motivations are still entirely directed by his lower unhealed nature, where there is no wisdom to be found. So this student will easily fall prey to the forces of darkness, for he has not addressed his own inner darkness. In time, his ego will become more dominant and his neglected inner wounds will demand an even more perfect mask. All that this novice is studying with regard to metaphysics and spiritual laws will simply feed the insatiable hunger of his mind and therefore only strengthen the mask. As a result, his search will become desperate and more focused on power, for his heart remains closed.

Some students may even develop brilliant insights, but without proper healing and alignment to the Divine these findings are merely pointless mind acrobatics. In extreme cases, people following this path end up becoming victims of the dark forces and find themselves in a very poor mental and emotional state, often confused, drug addicted, incapable of having stable loving relationships and, in the worst case, close to insanity and early death. Whereas the ones who follow the path of the light with perseverance and patience, and work through their inner healing, clearing their conditioning layer by layer and re-integrating their split-off aspects, will achieve a level of inner peace and balance unknown to the students of the occult.

In fact you could say that the student of the occult is serving his ego, whereas the student of the light transcends his ego and surrenders his lower will to the divine will. As Jesus said, 'Thy will, not mine, will be done'. Contrary to this, the motto of the occultists is 'Do as you please' (excerpt from the Thelema of Aleister Crowley). The latter maxim leads to inner and outer destruction. The path of the light shows the way to freedom and healing, and holds the key to the mystery of life. This is the path of love, while the path of the occult is severing the connection to love and aims solely for the satisfaction of the mind and ego, sustaining the mask and only feeding the lower nature. The hunger for power can become an obsession and, despite all effort and rituals, will never be satisfied. The disciple will then be left with the dreadful consequences of his actions, which are control, manipulation, humiliation, strict hierarchy and sarcasm. The path of love — 'The Way' — leads to greater Oneness, equality of all beings and harmlessness. The Path of Love leads to the Divine, where true power resides. When the ego is re-educated by love through healing and surrender to the Divine, Oneness with All That Is is achieved. In this Oneness, the human will becomes one with the divine will and miracles can occur. Whatever the aspirant to truth desires will begin to manifest. Interestingly, a true servant of the light will have few desires; therefore, when he expresses a rare wish the Divine will provide. Remember, a poor man is a man who has many desires. The student who acts in alignment with the Divine has learned to trust, and he walks in trust through life, knowing that the Divine supplies all of his needs.

Be vigilant with regard to the masters you serve. Be aware that the masters of darkness do not reveal their true face in the beginning. Often they will appear in disguise or even in the shape of a holy man.

Therefore learn discernment, for this is one of the most important tools on your journey through the jungle of spiritual truth, half-truth and temptations. There is never anything to fear, only more to love and learn. In the end, the darkness serves the light, when you have learned your lesson.

We sincerely ask that you cautiously consider a spiritual teacher and his teachings. If the teacher is not providing his students with a thorough emotional healing process, encourages dependency and does not insist on the importance of opening the heart to love and to becoming love, be vigilant and ask within your innermost soul if this is the path you wish to follow. Do these teachings serve the ego or do they heal your shadow and lead to inner liberation? Do these ideas only feed your curiosity and the hunger for knowledge or are they nourishing your heart and soul? The darkness wants your power and obedience, whereas the path of light leads to emotional, mental and spiritual maturity, true freedom and inner peace.

Wake up, people of the earth. Just because a group is calling itself spiritual does not necessarily mean this is the truth. Or just because someone is dressed in a white robe and recites holy words does not mean he is a saint. Use your heart, which knows and feels uneasy when the truth is bent and abused. Train in discernment and walk the Path of Love. Not all that is called spiritual is truly of the light. The spiritual scene is already infiltrated by the forces of darkness, but what a brilliant learning opportunity this is for studying discernment. There is never anything to fear, only more to learn and love. Remember, it is not the holy words that someone recites that are important; instead, how they act will tell who they are.

The darkness invites superiority, arrogance, sarcasm, self-centredness and selfishness, power over others, manipulation and control. The light leads you to equality, harmlessness, peace, love and Oneness. Look at the attributes a teaching invokes in you and you will easily find the distinction between the darkness and the divine light. The darkness has its driving force in preserving the ego and therefore the mask, which is illusionary and artificial, whereas the light heals the wounds that create the ego personality and aligns the personal will with the higher will. These are the spiritual foundations for a disciple on the path of light and, at the same time, the most significant distinction between these two opposing poles. Without emotional healing, the spiritual journey will not lead to inner freedom, for your main motivation remains unchanged and the ego is left in charge. Only when your soul overtakes the governance of your human personality, and you align to your divine self, will you find the road to true freedom.

50

BEFORE AND AFTER ENLIGHTENMENT

Prior to enlightenment, human beings strive to be someone special — someone important, while after enlightenment you are content to be no-one and it is enough just to be. Why is this so? Before enlightenment you are trapped in the polarities of the duality game, whereas when you are liberated your inner light is switched on and you have left behind the world of illusion — win and lose, right and wrong, good and bad, light and dark. For the first time, you begin to see the 'real world' and comprehend that who you believed you are, was in truth nothing but a concept. Your spiritual ego has made you out to be someone special, someone important. This yearning to be someone special is in fact telling you that you are not home. Only when all striving ends and you are content just to be — to be whatever the Divine wants you to be — are you truly free.

Beloveds, be clay in the hands of the Divine and do not fear to be nothing or nobody, because only he who has the trust and courage to be nothing can enter the 'real world' and begin to understand the sacred mystery of creation.

The majority of you are full of ideas of who you are, and these ideas and concepts stand between the Divine and you, hindering your true liberation. Let everything go — all concepts about you, the spiritual path, God and others, and surrender to the love of the Supreme Being. The greater your surrender, the more divine revelations can be given. Only through direct experience of the Divine can truth be understood. So be vigilant and observe your striving to be someone special, for this is an indicator of your incompletion and only highlights that you are still holding on to separation. When you have found inner freedom and become one with the Divine, there is no longer a need for explanation; all is then revealed and the desire to be someone special will forever cease.

The recognition of your own divinity can only occur in a space of absolute humility and through divine grace. You cannot achieve this state of being, regardless of how long you sit, pray and meditate. True enlightenment can only be given when a soul is ready to let go of all fear and concepts, and walks into the unknown naked, without the crutch of attained knowledge, in total trust and honesty, willing to enter the void. If you truly walk into the void, the unknown — where there is no longer ground beneath your feet, no walls to lean on, no light, no form, no knowing, nothing — then Source can take you home. This will be the most significant step on your spiritual journey, and it is impossible to describe in words the peace that follows the one who has truly surrendered.

Have the courage to surrender to the Divine all you think you are, every ounce of self-importance and self-centredness. Lay it on the altar of your heart and surrender it to Source. Only when you make space — total space — for God, can God fill you. If you are already filled, God cannot fill you. It is that simple. God cannot use you as long as you have not emptied yourself of the very last drop, until every fragment of fear is transformed and all concepts are dissolved in divine love. Your total surrender is the key. The pain you experience in the course of letting go can be understood as an alchemistic process of purification of your heart and soul, which is liberating you from illusion and allowing you to be consumed by the Divine. There is no other way. Any trace of self-importance is hindering the Divine to fully work through you.

51

THE BALANCE BETWEEN MALE AND FEMALE ENERGIES

Dear ones, we would like to turn our attention to another vital subject — the balance between male and female energies — for the significance of the balance of these two forces is not well known. To heighten your understanding, we wish to begin with a history lesson of a time on earth when all records were lost.

The great continent of Atlantis did exist and is not just a legend. The civilisation living there was highly advanced psychically and technologically. As with all civilisations, Atlantis experienced the rise, peak and then the fall of their culture. We are interested in examining more closely the fall of Atlantis and in particular the developments that unfolded in the thousands of years that followed the collapse.

You could say that the downfall of Atlantis was largely due to the predominant use of their extraordinary minds as well as their highly developed psychic abilities — in other words, the dominant use of their male energy. Through the abuse of these energies, the Atlanteans were in the process of destroying the whole planet, and it was decided that their civilisation would no longer be allowed to continue. The dramatic consequences of the downfall of Atlantis are referred to in the Bible and other ancient scripts as the Great Flood. Only a few survived, the majority being high-level initiates whose warnings of the approaching destruction had been ignored. They were powerless, had no means available to change the situation and with bottomless sadness they had to witness their whole civilisation vanishing. These survivors went to distant lands such as Egypt, Tibet and South America, where they began to teach the native people, who were living a primitive tribal life.

In analysing the reasons for the downfall of Atlantis, these survivors identified the one-sided male orientation and the abuse of psychic powers as being the main cause for the collapse of their civilisation. In order to avoid making the same mistake, they began to honour the Divine Feminine — women in general — and especially Mother Earth. Women at this time were perceived as sacred and powerful, for they were capable of establishing direct contact with the Divine through their strong heart connection. In addition to this attribute, they were gifted with the ability to bring new life into the world and also to fulfil the strong male sexual desires.

In the first centuries following Atlantis, the practice of honouring the Divine Feminine brought great blessings, and the new civilisations flourished. People lived a basic but very contented life in harmony, respect and love, and in connection with the Divine, with little of the previous highly advanced technology. This time was called The Golden Age. Unfortunately, during the millennia that followed, the original intent of honouring the female aspect of the Divine to offset the imbalance of the male was lost and this society became female dominated, which eventually took on the form of total domination over all men. In fact, it went so far that men were no longer regarded as human. They were seen as inferior to women and degraded to a sub-human level, only there for the purpose of giving sexual pleasure, ensuring the reproduction of the race and providing labour because of their advantage in physical strength. The female was considered to be superior.

In the history of the last few thousand years, you have clearly experienced the reverse of this story, where men have regarded themselves as superior to women. The fact that your world is in chaos and on the brink of global suicide visibly demonstrates the dangerous consequences of a society being predominantly male-orientated. These are the karmic consequences of an abuse from so long ago that you do not even have records of this time. Everything that is out of balance needs to be rebalanced over the course of time. This is cosmic law.

Let us return to the ancient time when the Goddess was worshipped. After a few thousand years the pendulum had swung to the other side and a revolution of the men began, because they had experienced enough injustice, oppression and submission and they demanded equal rights. But the women were used to their power and did not want to give up their superior position. Corruption and abuse of power had infiltrated all institutions of their society, including the spiritual leadership of the mystery schools. At this time, people believed that only a woman — a priestess — was able to connect with the Divine. Even the priests of the rare temples of the brotherhood were convinced of this theory. The revolution began within the male priesthood, filtered down through all levels of society and in the end involved the majority of men. With brutal violence came the destruction of the temples of the Goddess and eventually the overthrow of the matriarchate. After great devastation and chaos, the male priesthood took over the rulership.

However, these priests had not developed their own inner female side and were therefore unable to connect directly to the Divine. In fact, they needed the aid of women and, as a consequence, the practice of the temple priestess or temple whore became established in order to provide the priests and men of the ruling elite with a connection to the Divine. This indirect form of contact to the Divine was facilitated with the help of sexual union. The priestess connected through her Higher Self to the Divine while performing the sexual act and thus transmitted the spiritual energy to the man. For several thousand years, throughout many cultures, these rituals were performed as an 'indirect way' to honour the Goddess.

There the abuse of women began and with it a major decline in consciousness. These practices were built upon the false assumption that only a female can have direct contact to the Divine, which is not the truth. The truth is that the female aspect of a man or a woman, physically represented through the heart, is able to connect to the Divine. This fundamental misunderstanding influenced all cultures and subsequently all religions that were founded on this flawed belief. Many thousands of years later, the cult of the Goddess was totally eradicated, and the predominantly male-orientated religions and leadership that still direct life on earth today became the prime influences on mainstream thinking.

In some of the ancient prophecies it is said that now is the time of the return of the Goddess. This is indeed the truth, but not to change a one-sided male-orientated society on the brink of global destruction back to a one-sided female society. The Goddess returns to bring back balance. To repeat the mistakes of history would make little sense. History has shown that civilisations only flourished when the male and female energies of its inhabitants, ruling class and priesthood were in balance. Any imbalance to one side or the other always leads to destruction, slavery, humiliation and great injustice, and in the end to decline. We want you to learn from history and understand its imperative lessons.

There is a male and female side in all human beings, and both aspects need to be developed and balanced in order for a person to reach their full potential and connect with the Divine. If you are solely orientated by your female energies, your life and spirituality often becomes ungrounded and you may experience difficulties in achieving your goals. On the other hand, when your male aspect is too dominant, there is the danger that the sacred teachings are only absorbed by the mind without appropriate inner transformation and action. Then you will be someone who talks about spiritual knowledge, because you have understood it intellectually, but not made it to your own by living what you believe. In fact, you only borrow the words from others who have found inner freedom but you still remain a slave to your mind.

Everyone needs to have a deep look within, assess the balance between their male and female energies, and work on developing both sides in order to bring them into a healthy equilibrium. The spiritual heart is a portal to the Divine but is also representative of your female side and receives wisdom and inspiration, whereas your male aspect is meant to bring these ideas into manifestation through living a life according to the guidance of the heart. The male and the female need each other. Only through working together in harmony can your civilisation make the leap into the next Golden Age.

In all men and women incarnated today there still live the remnants and memories of a long-forgotten past. In some women, this can take on the form of resentment towards men in a sexual manner, because these women hold the unresolved painful memories of their lives as temple whores or experiences of total submission without rights and power. Alternatively, some men, especially very male-orientated men, unconsciously hold deep-seated suspicions towards women, for all their cells still remember the final phase of the matriarchate, when men experienced great injustice and hurt. These men find it difficult to truly open their hearts and trust a woman. In all relationships they need to stay in control, by either being emotionally unavailable or hurting and putting their partners down for fear of losing power.

It is time that these deep wounds between men and women begin to heal and that every individual balances their male and female energies within. Only then can outer balance come to your society, governments, churches, temples and businesses. As always, everything starts from within, which is the sacred principle of the Spiral, the ancient symbol of the Goddess and the Divine Mother. Do not believe that the Goddess is dominantly female. Nothing could be further from the truth. The Goddess may express herself through female attributes and form, yet she represents the perfect balance of male and female within herself. Many of the ancient cultures and their religious teachings were well aware of this fact. You only have to look at the Goddess Kali, who represents one of the aspects of the Goddess — the destroyer in Hindu culture. This aspect of destruction would in western mythology be classified as purely male.

The Goddess is returning, yet she comes in perfect balance to bring with her all of her aspects such as nurturing, patience, love, compassion, mentoring, preserving, sensuality — and also destruction of what is out of alignment with truth. She is teaching you to develop and balance all of who you are. Respect each other's differences, see the beauty in these differences and help each other grow to be truly whole. A whole being is someone who has healed and mastered all of the four bodies, balanced the inner female and male aspects and passed various spiritual initiations to stand in his true shining light.

Develop understanding when you see someone acting in an unwise or even hurtful manner, regardless of whether this behaviour is influenced by a predominantly male or female aspect. Know that this behaviour, which is often creating havoc, is caused by great pain and fear, derived from records of the past that are still lingering in their subconscious. Do not judge others; instead help them to heal with understanding and love. Love is the great healer. Love is who you are.

The goal for every person, whether incarnated in a male or female body, is to become totally balanced within, aligned with the Divine and firmly grounded to the earth. Only then will the promised Golden Age fully blossom, and peace, understanding, true respect and forgiveness come to all men and women on earth.

52

THE GREAT SHIFT

A decade ago, the year 2012 became the focus of global attention as the year for the prophesied global shift, as the Mayan Calendar ended on 21.12.2012. Many of you were disappointed, as seemingly no major visible changes occurred. Yet wise men and women knew that a decade or even several decades might be necessary for a global transformation of this scale. This shift can be compared to the birth of a child, where the mother has to go through the painful labour until her body and the baby are ready for the birth. And the same applies with all changes happening on planet earth. You are in the midst of the labour pains of a new world being born. You are witnessing chaos, uncertainty, the collective shadow of whole nations arising, as well as your own shadow becoming visible.

Several native tribes and the ancient prophecies also speak about this special time. The names under which this event is described do not matter; they vary, depending on the culture and the time frame in which they were received. However, what all of these prophecies have in common is that they describe a major cataclysm that will fundamentally change the face of humanity and the earth forever.

It does not matter whether you call this time 'the second coming', 'the reappearance of Christ', 'the rebirth of the Lord Maitreya', 'the coming of the Messiah', 'the end of time' or anything else. What is important is that there has been for hundreds of years, in some cases even thousands of years, a common sentiment in the hearts and minds of the seers around the globe that these events are about to unfold. These prophets all agreed that, at approximately the same time, a massive event will change humanity and planet earth.

Let us have a closer look at these changes and the actual reason for them. Change is nothing new, and planet earth has gone through countless transformations since its creation and will continue to do so. Yet you are participating in and witnessing one of the greatest and most unique transformations a planet has ever experienced, and this is the exact reason why you are all here. Some say earth is moving into a different spectrum of frequency, into the full alignment with the Galactic Core, the centre of the galaxy. Others see the increase in strength in the solar eruptions as a possible reason for a tremendous impact on earth and there are many other theories surrounding this subject.

We do not wish to get involved in this kind of speculation, and would only like to say that the earth as you know it will be transformed, as too will you as human beings. During the course of this book we have explained to you that a New Earth is emerging and we also said that you cannot take anything with you into this new world that is not in alignment with love, peace and truth. With the teachings in this book we have endeavoured to prepare you for these events, which have already begun to unfold, by explaining in the simplest terms possible various topics to deepen your understanding of the massive transformation that lies ahead. Humanity is receiving a new programming so to speak, that will affect the way you perceive yourselves, others and the world. Old limited perceptions will simply fall away, and after a period of inner and outer chaos you will adjust to this new way of being and live in greater alignment with your Creator.

We have tried to explain to you who we are, but we still sense that many of you find it difficult to comprehend the truth about our identity. Therefore, for the sake of simplicity, call us Love. The purpose of our communication with you lies solely in awakening you to your true divine nature and preparing you for the coming shift. Your planet is undergoing a massive transformation that is becoming more visible through the increase in the number of earthquakes, tsunamis and volcanic eruptions.

Mother Earth is freeing herself from all negative imprints that human beings have left through the denial of their divine nature and the ignorance of the universal law of the Oneness of all beings. This kind of inferior consciousness expresses itself in war, greed, power abuse, lies, suppression, control and manipulation of others and the total exploitation of this beautiful host planet. Earth is a living being — she is an expression of divine consciousness just as you are. Imagine if someone were to rip your organs out, destroy your bloodstream, tear off your skin, pull your eyes out, hack off your limbs and worse. This is exactly what human beings are doing to Mother Earth.

For instance, mining of precious metals, oil and gas drilling, pollution of air, water and soil, are destroying the vital functions of your Mother. Each one of these metals, crystals and layers of coal, oil and gas has a specific function within the body of Mother Earth, not unlike the different organs of your physical body, your lymphatic system and blood circulation, which ensure that your body can properly function. Your environment is so severely polluted that it is already affecting all life forms on your planet. Do you really believe the increasing rate of illnesses, such as cancer, has no relation to your inner and outer pollution? With the term 'inner pollution', we are referring to the pollution of your mind and your emotional fields. The outer pollution of your environment is closely linked to your inner pollution. In fact, your environmental disasters are a direct visible consequence and outer manifestation of the pollution within.

Earth is in such a desperate state that she needs to act in order to survive. Few can imagine the endless patience and unconditional love Mother Gaia, as the earth is known by the ancient tribes, has for her children; however, she has come to a point where she needs to take action. So she has already begun to move to free herself from the energetic imprints of a history of violence, war, greed, disregard, betrayal and self-centredness, which are written into the different layers of the earth. Earth is a record holder similar to a computer disk, storing memory. For eons, graciously and in divine patience, earth has witnessed and permitted these deeds of lower consciousness. Now her patience has ceased and she is ridding herself of these dark energies.

You could use the analogy of a serious disease such as cancer that is now affecting her overall wellbeing. What would you do when you receive the diagnosis of cancer? Wouldn't you begin to cleanse your body and try to find the most effective treatment to heal this illness in order to survive? This is exactly what Mother Earth is doing: she is cleansing her body. This cleansing process has its outer expression in the form of major earthquakes, tsunamis, volcanic eruptions and other disturbances. The general human interpretation of these events is 'catastrophe'. Yet from a higher point of consciousness it is a healing process, and the way you live and how you treat this wonderful planet is the true catastrophe.

The way this healing process of Mother Earth will play out has a lot to do with you. In the last few decades there have been many warnings that the ruling elite of your planet has played down or simply ignored. You are already experiencing the horrific consequences of what can happen when you do not listen to the warnings of scientists, environmental groups and the elders of the tribes, who have predicted this kind of calamity for a long time.

There is not much time left to prevent further catastrophic events unfolding in different places around the globe. You need to realise that you still have a choice. Stand up and call for an end to the exploitation and pollution of your sacred Mother. If this were to happen, the effects of the changes naturally occurring on the surface of the earth and within would be less traumatic. Besides healing and restoring the sacred and vital functions of Mother Earth, there is another purpose for this cleansing, and this is of a spiritual nature. Mother Earth is transforming herself and aligning with the galactic core, which implies a dramatic increase in her frequency.

Earth is going through this transformation regardless of your continued exploitation. Your actions only determine the impact these changes will have on you. You need to comprehend that there are, at any given moment in time, a multitude of possible futures. This can be compared to the large variety of TV channels that are available to you. For instance, you are watching TV, but, depending on which channel you choose, you will view a different scene on the screen. Your choice of channel stands in direct relation to your frequency. When you choose to *Be Love*, respectful to self, others and Mother Earth, and express harmlessness, peace and truth, then the manifestations of outer events occurring will differ vastly compared to what will transpire if you choose self-centredness and separation thinking and your heart remains closed.

You cannot bring this sacred transformation to a halt, yet your decisions will determine the effects the shift will have on humanity.

You can still choose a less dramatic scenario by being love and living the true virtues of life. These virtues are truth, love, peace, compassion, kindness, patience, integrity, forgiveness, harmlessness and sharing. You can also call this Unity consciousness.

All of the disasters which have already occurred can be understood as a wake-up call to humanity, a call for the opening of your hearts and the realisation that no-one can forever abuse the earth without serious consequences. These events may even bring you closer to who you really are, so that you comprehend that you are all one — one consciousness, one being in different appearances. You may realise, when someone in another part of the world is suffering, that you are all suffering and that you need to extend your helping hands, or at least fold your hands in prayer if you are unable to directly stretch them out.

Not only is earth going through this cleansing and healing process, which implies a dimensional shift — a shift in consciousness — you as human beings are also experiencing this transformation. This whole book, as with others, is here to prepare you for these events. A new light is emerging on earth which is so extraordinary, that never before in human history has anything like it happened. The almighty presence of the Divine is descending onto the earth plane to bring a light brighter than a million suns, dissolving all illusions that have kept you spellbound for eons. Your human mind cannot imagine the magnitude of the event that is gradually unfolding. All governments that bend the truth, all systems enslaving humanity, all manipulation, lies and control, will fall. Nothing that is not at peace and aligned to truth and love can withstand the light of the Divine.

Yet the destruction of the old systems of lies is only one aspect of these unfolding events. There is another, more pleasant, facet to all of this, namely that humanity is receiving an influx of light that will expand its consciousness in a way that only few can imagine. For many of you, it may appear as if you are waking up from a very long dream — a nightmare in fact. First, you will feel unfamiliar with these changes and it will take time to get used to your new way of life. You can be rest assured that you are helped on every step along the way. Know that you are not alone.

Please, do not fear these events. Instead, see the greater picture and understand that it is the purest essence of love pouring onto this plane directly from the Heart of God. The result of this transformation will be so beautiful that it is almost impossible to imagine.

We would like to add some thoughts regarding the time frame of this shift. Precise dates in the prophecies should not be taken too literally (as being the exact time in which these events will unfold). There is certainly a tremendous influx of light, and at this particular time celestial portals are opening and higher frequencies flooding planet earth. This will initially influence the more subtle levels of individual consciousness as well as the finer layers of Mother Earth. The manifestations of these higher energy alignments on the earth plane will unfold in their own time.

So do not expect a world of peace to emerge nor wait for the earth's total destruction on a certain date. Everything is a process, and takes time in the third dimension. People will also experience these events very differently depending on their level of consciousness and degree of inner healing. For some, they will bring an incredible spiritual opening, while for others who have not yet begun their inner journey, the increase in higher frequency will bring to the fore aspects of their shadow. This effect should not be understood as punishment, but instead as an opportunity to face what has lain dormant for so long.

The best way to prepare for this time, which is now, is to live centred in your heart. Be love and be at peace, speak the truth and leave the rest up to the Divine. Know that you are loved.

53

WE ARE LOVE

Dear ones, this is our final endeavour to make known to you who we are, to ease the minds of those still finding it difficult to understand who is speaking to you. Know that we are The One Who Is All That Is. We are The Formless birthing all forms — we are The Nameless One who gave all of you your names. We are The Nothingness who gave life to all and everything. We Are The One Who Was Never Born And Can Never Die.

During eons of creation, you have given us many names and these names have changed as consciousness has risen and fallen. Consciousness on this planet, as in all of creation, is always following the pattern of rise and fall, as does your breath — the out breath follows the in breath. You draw in life force with your in breath and release it when you exhale. These waves of consciousness — the ups and downs — create the divine game, the divine dance between the shadow and the light, also called Lila or Maya, the play of illusion.

Do not fear the shadow dance from within or the darkness from outside, but also do not fear the magnificence of your own light — which is brighter than the light of a million suns — calling you home. Embrace all within as well as everything on the outside. Know there is nowhere to go except into your heart. All answers you are desperately looking for are written there in the golden letters of the sacred language of love and have been waiting for you for eons. Only love can decipher its meaning.

Understand that we do not need a name. Our only wish is that you understand that you are love and love is the highest power. In fact, power serves love! If you need a name, call us Love or the Heart of God. Be Love, for Love Is All That There Is, All That There Ever Was — and All That There Ever Will Be.

ROSE OF LOVE

My heart
Flames of Light
Flashing
Shooting up
My crown

Light explosions
The Eye of RA
My crystal crown

I AM invisible
Invulnerable

I
Emerge from the skies
Deep inside
The Core of the Earth
My roots

Birthed
Myself
Into form

A trillion light speed
Beyond
Your
Wildest imagination

I am born again
For
The first time
In my true Glory

In grace
I AM
The Mother of all Life
Descending

Oh
Crown of Life
I AM
Your Glory

I am
The Nameless One

That
Gave all of you
Your name

Rose of Light

My heart
Explodes
Bursting
Into lightning

A myriad
Thunderstorms of Love
I AM

Who
Ever can grasp
Who
AM I

So white
So purified

My pearl
Was born
Under pressure

Uncounted tears
Had been
My
Lives

The past
Just dust
Dust
In the wind

Now
I AM the wind

Thunderstorm
And
Lightning
My rose
Eternal love

Birthing light
My thousand fold
Lotus crown

Who
Can ever bear
The love
I AM

So
I
Hide
Hide
And
Hide
My light

Stay invisible
In divine secrecy

The Mother of all Life
Hides
Behind
A silent smile

BEYOND CREATION

Beyond creation
That is where
I'm coming from

Stillness is my robe
A silent smile
My single jewel

I am love
Tenderness
Healing all wounds

I am love
Power and strength
The glory of The Nameless One

I am love
In pure simplicity I AM
Silent love

Do you remember the place
Where no movement is

Where all self-importance
Loses it's importance

Nothing
I have to prove
No image to create

In Silent simplicity
I AM THAT I AM

No movement
No creation
No expression
That is what I AM

Beyond creation
That is where
I'm coming from

Air too fine to breathe
Silence too exquisite to be named

Dive into
The secret realms of silence

Be
Be who you are

Your heart is breaking
Listening to my song

Your heart is all
I am longing for

Your heart is longing
Just for me

The Return — Peace

Labyrinth of Life

ABOUT THE AUTHOR

Mirjam was born in 1963 in the French part of Switzerland, grew up in Germany, lived in France and immigrated to Australia in 2002, where she now lives with her family.

Her professional background includes glass design, art therapy, Gestalt therapy and she is also trained as an end of life consultant.

Mirjam worked as an artist, writer, meditation teacher and counselor in various countries around the world. She has a special interest supporting children and adults facing death, cancer and depression and is a passionate advocate of love in action.

www.silentsmile.com

www.ingramcontent.com/pod-product-compliance
Lightning Source LLC
Chambersburg PA
CBHW051418290426
44109CB00016B/1350